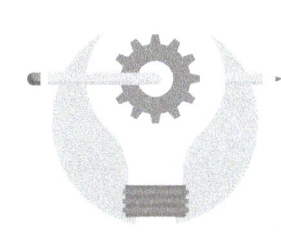

PARCC TEST PREP

GRADE 3

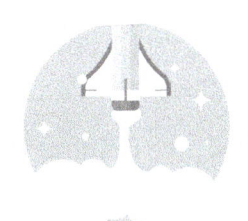

ENGLISH LANGUAGE ARTS

Origins Publications

We help students develop their higher-order thinking skills while also improving their chances of admission into gifted and accelerated-learner programs.

Our goal is to unleash and nurture the genius in every student. We do this by offering educational and test prep materials that are fun, challenging and provide a sense of accomplishment.

Please contact us with any questions.

info@originspublications.com

Copyright © 2018 by Origins Publications

Written and Edited by: PARCC ELA Test Prep Team

All rights reserved. This book or any portion thereof may not be reproduced or used in any manner whatsoever without the express written permission of the publisher.

ISBN: 13: 978-1-948255-05-9

PARCC® is a registered trademark of PARCC Inc (the Partnership for the Assessment of Readiness for College and Careers, Inc), which is not affiliated with Origins Publications. PARCC has not endorsed the contents of this book.

Origins Publications
New York, NY, USA
Email:info@originspublications.com

TABLE OF CONTENTS

Introduction 4
How To Use This Book 5
Test Prep Tips 6

Reading: Literature 7
Ask & Answer Questions Using Text Evidence (3.RL.1.1) 8
Recount Stories & Determine Theme (3.RL.1.2) 13
Describe Characters & Explain Their Actions (L3.RL.1.3) 17
Determine Word Meaning In Context (3.RL.2.4) 21
Identify & Understand Parts Of Texts (3.RL.2.5) 23
Identify Point Of View of Self & Author/Characters (3.RL.2.6) 26
Identify How Illustrations Convey Information (3.RL.3.7) 29
Compare & Contrast Narratives (3.RL.3.9) 32

Reading: Information 36
Ask & Answer Questions Using Text Evidence (3.RI.1.1) 37
Determine Main Idea & Explain Key Details (3.RI.1.2) 41
Describe & Understand Relationships Between Ideas (3.RI.1.3) 45
Determine Domain-Specific Word Meaning in Context (3.RI.2.4) 49
Use Text Features & Search Tools (3.RI.2.5) 53
Identify Point Of View of Self & Author (3.RI.2.6) 56
Use & Understand Information In Illustrations (3.RI.3.7) 60
Describe & Make Connections In Text (3.RI.3.8) 63
Compare And Contrast Key Points In Two Texts (3.RI.3.9) 67

Language 70
Demonstrate Command of Grammar & Usage (3 .L.1.1) 71
Know Capitalization, Punctuation & Spelling (3 .L.1.2) 73
Use Appropriate Language Conventions (3 .L.2.3) 75
Determine Meaning of Unknown Word/s in Context (3 .L.3.4) 78
Understand Word Relationships and Nuances in Meaning (3 .L.3.5) 80
Know Academic/Domain-Specific Words (3 .L.3.6) 82

Answer Key and Explanations 85

Practice Tests 97
Practice Test One 99
Practice Test One Answer Key & Explanations 123

   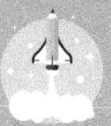      

INTRODUCTION

The PARCC Assessments

The PARCC Assessments (Partnership for Assessment of Readiness for College and Careers) are important tests designed to assess whether students are meeting the rigorous Common Core State Standards that have been implemented in schools across America. These standards, or learning goals, outline what students in each grade should learn each year. They emphasize just how important the new goals are: they can help show whether students are on the right track to college and beyond, even when the students are years from those life stages.

PARCC is a consortium of US states which cooperate to develop and improve the PARCC Assessments.

PARCC English Language Arts (ELA) Test

The PARCC ELA assessment is designed to determine whether students have mastered grade level appropriate reading and writing skills. Like the Common Core State Standards, PARCC assessments focus on higher level critical thinking skills, problem solving, analysis, and real-world application.

The PARCC ELA assessments are given annually in grades 3-11. The assessments are given during a 30-day window that ends about 75% of the way through the school year, and are administered in either computer-based or paper-based formats.

Each ELA assessment is divided into three sessions, called "units."

Unit 1: Literary Analysis Task: Students read 2 literature passages and answer questions. Students write 1 'literary analysis' essay based on the texts. Students read one short literary or informational text and answer questions.

Unit 2: Research Simulation Task: Students read 1 short narrative passage and answer questions. Students write 1 'narrative' essay based on the text. Students read 1 long informational passage or possibly a paired set of passages (if 4th grade or above) and answer questions.

Unit 3: Narrative Writing Task: Students read 3 informational passages (one of these could be presented as multimedia) and answer questions. Students write 1 'research simulation' essay that synthesizes and/or compares and contrasts the texts.

PARCC assessments are timed. The amount of time provided varies by grade. For Grade 3, units 1 and 3 are 90 minutes and unit 2 is 75 minutes. For Grades 4-5, all units are 90 minutes.

Question Format on PARCC ELA Assessments

There are three major question types on PARCC ELA exams.

Evidence-Based Selected Response: This is the most common question type, and it combines a traditional multiple choice question with a question asking students to select evidence from the text.

Tech-Enhanced Constructed Response: Students use use technology (drag and drop, cut and paste, move items to show relationship) to demonstrate critical thinking, analysis, and comprehension abilities. Students may be asked to select pieces of text to support a claim, check each box that could be a correct response to the question, drag and drop steps into the correct order, etc.

Range of Prose Constructed Response: These questions verify that students have understood a text(s) and can communicate that understanding through written expression, demonstrating knowledge of language and conventions.

HOW TO USE THIS BOOK

The objective of this book is to provide students, educators, and parents with practice materials focused on the core skills needed to help students succeed on the PARCC assessment.

A student will fare better on an assessment when s/he has practiced and mastered the skills measured by the test. A student also excels when s/he is familiar with the format and structure of the test. This book helps students do both. Students can review key material by standard through doing the skill-building exercises, as well as take practice tests to become accustomed to how the content is presented and to enhance test-taking skills. By test day, students will feel confident and be adequately prepared to do his or her best.

This Book Includes:

- 196 skill-building exercises organised by standard in order to help students learn and review concepts in the order that they will likely be presented in the classroom. These worksheets also help identify weaknesses, and highlight and strengthen the skills needed to excel on the actual exam. A variety of question types are included in the worksheets to help students build skills in answering questions in multiple formats, so they don't get tripped up by perplexing or unfamiliar question types on test day.

- Practice test materials that are based on the official PARCC assessments released by the test administrator, and include similar question types and the same rigorous content found on the official assessments. By using these materials, students will become familiar with the types of items (including Technology Enhanced Constructed Response questions, presented in a paper based format) they may see on the real test.

- Answer keys with detailed explanations to help students not make the same mistakes again. These explanations help clear up common misconceptions and indicate how students might arrive at an answer to a question.

- Answer keys also identify the standard/s that the question is assessing. If a student is having difficulty in one area, encourage the student to improve in that area by practicing the specific set of skills in the workbook.

- Test prep tips to help students approach the test strategically and with confidence.

   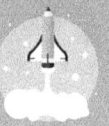     

TEST PREP TIPS

First of all, remind your student to pay attention in class throughout the year, asking questions as needed on homework and classwork. The Language Arts curriculum should follow the exact standards and skills that will be tested on the end-of-year assessment.

One of the best ways to prepare for a reading test is by—of course—reading. In the months leading up to the test, have your student read a certain amount of pages or minutes weekly from a book that she enjoys. Reading consistently will improve your student's reading comprehension and enhance her vocabulary, two skills that are crucial to success on the exam.

Another extremely effective strategy is to practice, practice, practice. Have your student work on practice questions and complete at several full length practice tests. Our practice test is a great place to start.

However, simply answering the questions and then moving on will not yield much improvement. If your student misses a question, discuss why the correct answer is indeed correct. Come up with alternate approaches to this question type that may work better in the future. Have your student explain her answer to each question. This gives you the opportunity to reinforce logical thinking and correct misconceptions as needed. Plus, it's good practice for finding evidence to support a claim, perhaps the key skill on ELA reading assessments.

Prior to the test, encourage students to get a solid night of sleep and eat a nourishing breakfast.

For children, avoiding test anxiety is very important, so be sure to avoid over-emphasizing the test or inadvertently causing your student to feel excessive stress or pressure.

In addition, **teach your student general test-taking strategies such as the following:**

Narrow down your answer choices by using process of elimination. This involves crossing out obviously wrong answers to increase your chances of finding the correct answer.

If you get stuck on a question, skip it and come back to it after answering easier questions.

Remember that no one is expected to answer every single correction correctly. Don't panic when you get stuck on a question. Take a deep breath and remember that you are intelligent and prepared.

If you follow the tips here, your student should be well on her way to a stress-free and successful performance on this important assessment.

READING: LITERATURE

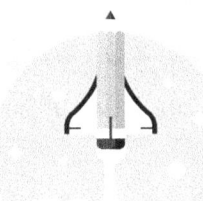  

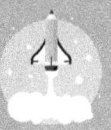

ASK & ANSWER QUESTIONS USING TEXT EVIDENCE

RL.1.1: Ask and answer questions to demonstrate understanding of a text, referring explicitly to the text as the basis for the answers.

Directions: Read the passage and answer the questions that follow.

Passage 1: The Cheeses That Ran Away
by Clifton Johnson

1   There was a man of Gotham who filled a sack with cheeses and started off for Nottingham market to sell them. He carried the sack on his back, and when he became tired he sat down by the wayside to rest. Thus he went on until he reached the summit of the last hill he had to climb before he came to Nottingham bridge.

2   There he rested, and when he rose to continue his journey a cheese slipped out of the sack and rolled down the hill toward the bridge.

3   "Ah! Mr. Cheese," said the man, "so you can run to market alone, can you? I wish I had known that before. It would have saved me the trouble of carrying you. Well, then, if you can go to market alone, so can the other cheeses, and I will send them along after you."

4   So he laid down his sack, took out the cheeses, and one by one rolled them down the hill. As the last one spun down the road he shouted, "I charge you all to meet me at the market-place."

5   Some of the cheeses went into one bush, and some went into another bush, but the man did not notice that, and he trudged on cheerfully to the market expecting the cheeses would meet him there. All day long he loitered about the market, and as evening approached he began to inquire among his friends and neighbors and other men if they had seen his cheeses come to the market.

6   "Who should bring them?" asked one of the market-men.

7   "Nobody," replied the man of Gotham. "They would bring themselves. They know the way well enough."

1. This question has two parts. First, answer Part A. Then, answer Part B.
Part A
Where does the man believe his cheeses are going?
    A. He thinks they're going into the bushes.
    B. He thinks they're running away.
    C. He thinks they're meeting him at the marketplace.
    D. He thinks they're going back home.

Part B
Which piece of evidence from the passage best supports your answer to Part A?
- **A.** "Well, then, if you can go to market alone, so can the other cheeses, and I will send them along after you." (Paragraph 3)
- **B.** "So he laid down the sack, took out his cheeses, and one by one rolled them down the hill." (Paragraph 4)
- **C.** "There was a man of Gotham who filled a sack with cheeses and started off for Nottingham market to sell them." (Paragraph 1)
- **D.** "Then he rested, and when he rose to continue his journey a cheese slipped out of the sack and rolled down the hill toward the bridge." (Paragraph 2)

2. What is one piece of evidence from the story that gives you a clue that the cheeses will likely not find their way to market?
    - **A.** "As the last one spun down the road he shouted, 'I charge you all to meet me at the market-place.'"
    - **B.** "Some of the cheeses went into one bush, and some went into another bush, but the man did not notice that…"
    - **C.** "Then he rested, and when he rose to continue his journey a cheese slipped out of the sack and rolled down the hill toward the bridge."
    - **D.** ""Ah! Mr. Cheese," said the man, "so you can run to market alone, can you? I wish I had known that before."

3. What detail from the text tells why the man rolled his cheeses down the hill after the first cheese escaped?

_____

_____

_____

4. What do you think will happen next in the story?
    - **A.** The cheeses will come to the marketplace and the man will sell them.
    - **B.** The man will never find his cheeses.
    - **C.** The man will find out that one of the other villagers took his cheeses.
    - **D.** The cheeses will come to the marketplace too late.

READING: LITERATURE

   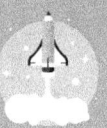      

Passage 2: The Kettle That Would Not Walk
by Clifton Johnson

1   One day a Gotham man was getting ready to go to market, and his wife said to him, "Husband, we need a new iron kettle for the fireplace. Don't fail to buy one."

2   So the man bought a kettle at Nottingham, and toward evening he took it on his arm and started for home. But the kettle was heavy, and at length his arm grew tired with carrying it and he set it down. While he was resting he noticed that the kettle had three legs. "What a pity I did not see those legs before!" cried the man. "Here you have three legs and I have but two, and yet I have been carrying you. 'Twere fairer that you had carried me. Well, you shall take me the rest of the way, at least."

3   Then he seated himself in the kettle and said, "Now, go on; I am all ready;" but the kettle stood stock still on its three legs and would not move.

4   "Ah!" said the man, "you are stubborn, are you? You want me to keep on carrying you, I suppose; but I shall not. I will tell you the way and you can stay where you are until you get ready to follow me."

5   So he told the kettle where he lived and how to get there, and then off the man went. When he reached home his wife asked him where the kettle was.

6   "Oh, it will be along in good time," he replied.

7   "And what do you mean by that?" said she.

8   "Why," said he, "the kettle I bought has three legs, and was better able to walk here from Nottingham market than I who have but two legs. Yet I never noticed it had legs until I was nearly here. Then I told it to walk the rest of the way itself, for I would carry it no farther."

9   "Where did you leave it?" asked the wife.

10   "You need not be anxious," responded the man.

11   "I told it the way, and it will be along in good time, as I said before."

12   "And where did you leave it?" again asked the wife.

13   "At Gotham bridge," he replied.

14   She was not so sure about its coming as he was and she hurried off to get it, and when she brought it home the man said, "I am glad you have it safe, wife, for I have been thinking while you were gone that it might have taken a notion to walk back to Nottingham if we had left it alone there in the road much longer."

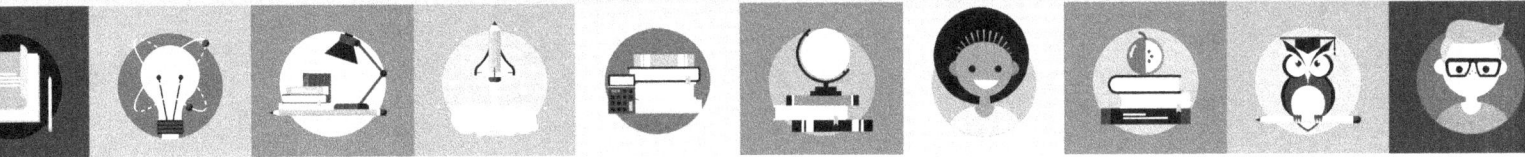

5. The man and his wife have different opinions about leaving the kettle to walk home on its own. Describe the man's opinion and the wife's opinion. Use details from the passage to support your answer.

   Man's Opinon:

   _____
   _____
   _____

   Supporting Detail:

   _____
   _____
   _____

   Wife's Opinon:

   _____
   _____
   _____

   Supporting Detail:

   _____
   _____
   _____

6. Which detail from the text explains why the man believes the kettle should carry him instead?

   _____
   _____
   _____
   _____

7. In what way are the cheeses from Passage 1 and the kettle from Passage 2 similar?
   A. They both refuse to walk.
   B. They both disobey their owners.
   C. They both run away.
   D. They both are sold in a marketplace in the end.

READING: LITERATURE

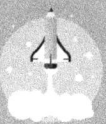

8. This question has two parts. First, answer Part A. Then, answer Part B.

Part A

What sentence describes the woman's feelings at the end of the passage?

    A. She agrees with the man that the kettle will come home eventually.

    B. She thinks the kettle will walk back to Nottingham.

    C. She doesn't think the kettle will come home.

    D. She thinks the man is lying and never really bought a kettle.

Part B

What happens as a result of the woman's feelings in Part A?

    A. The woman gets mad at the man.

    B. The woman goes to get the kettle and bring it home.

    C. The woman tells the man to go get the kettle.

    D. The woman and the man wait for the kettle to arrive.

RECOUNT STORIES & DETERMINE THEME

RL.1.2. Recount stories, including fables, folktales, and myths from diverse cultures; determine the central message, lesson, or moral and explain how it is conveyed through key details in the text.

Directions: Read the passage and answer the questions that follow.

Passage 1: The Ant and the Grasshopper
Adapted from the fable by Aesop

1   In a field one summer's day a Grasshopper was hopping about, chirping and singing to its heart's content. An Ant passed by, carrying an ear of corn he was taking to the nest.

2   "Why not come and chat with me," said the Grasshopper, "instead of working in that way?"

3   "I am helping to lay up food for the winter," said the Ant," and recommend you do the same."

4   "Why bother about winter?" said the Grasshopper. "We have got plenty of food at present." But the Ant went on its way and continued its work.

5   A few days later, the Grasshopper was playing a game with his friends when the Ant passed by, again bearing food.

6   "Take a break and come play with us," the Grasshopper urged the Ant.

7   "Winter is coming soon," the Ant told him. "I have to ensure my family has enough food."

8   "We have many days left until winter," said the Grasshopper. "All that work isn't necessary." But the Ant ignored the Grasshopper and continued its work.

9   When the winter came, the Grasshopper had no food and found itself dying of hunger. Every day, he saw the ants distributing the corn and grain they had collected in the summer.

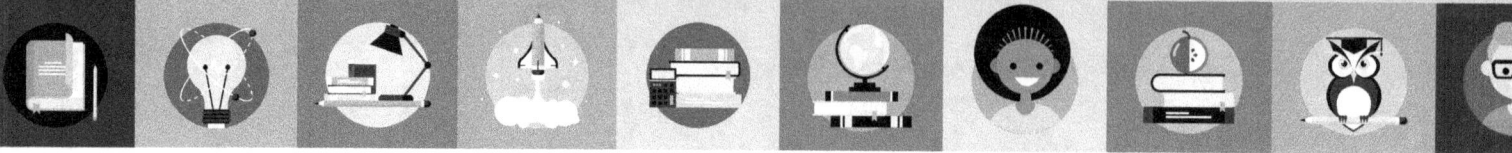

1. Using the details from "The Ant and the Grasshopper," complete the sequence of events below.

(1) The Grasshopper asks the Ant to chat with him, but the Ant says he is putting away food for the winter.

(2) _____

(3) The Grasshopper again sees the Ant and asks him to come play with him, but the Ant says he has to make sure his family has enough food for winter.

(4) The Grasshopper says there is plenty of time left until winter and the Ant's work isn't necessary.

(5) _____

2. What is a main lesson in the fable "The Ant and the Grasshopper?"

_____
_____
_____
_____

3. Which detail helps to convey the fable's lesson?
    A. "An Ant passed by, bearing along carrying an ear of corn he was taking to the nest."
    B. "'Winter is coming soon,' the Ant told him."
    C. "In a field one summer's day a Grasshopper was hopping about, chirping and singing to its heart's content."
    D. "When the winter came, the Grasshopper had no food and found itself dying of hunger."

4. Why doesn't the Grasshopper want to work like the Ant? Use information from the passage to support your answer.

_____
_____
_____
_____
_____
_____

READING: LITERATURE

Passage 2: The Story of Icarus
Adapted from Greek mythology

1   A very long time ago on the island of Crete, a father and his son Icarus were imprisoned in a cave high above the sea. They had been imprisoned because the father was an extremely talented inventor, and the greedy King wanted the father to work only for him.

2   As Icarus became a teenager, he began to want a life of his own outside of the cave.

3   Icarus' father asked the King if he could let Icarus go, but the King refused his request.

4   When the father saw the disappointed face of his son Icarus, he knew that he must find a way for Icarus to escape. He gazed out of the cave and noticed seagulls flying high over the waves. At that moment, he had an idea.

5   For many days, the father and son collected seagull feathers. The father used metal frames to create two pairs of man-sized wings, and he attached the seagull feathers with candle wax.

6   On the day they planned to leave, the father reminded his son, "Icarus, remember not to fly too close to the sun. If you do, the wax will melt and you'll lose your feathers. Just follow my path." Icarus agreed.

7   As the father and son started to fly, Icarus loved the freedom he felt. He watched the seagulls soar higher and higher and decided to follow them.

8   "Icarus, stop!" yelled his father. "If you fly too high, the wax will melt. Not so high, Icarus!"

9   But Icarus didn't listen. As he flew even higher, he started to feel the wax melting down his arms. He saw his feathers slipping off and falling into the ocean. Icarus tried to fly lower, but it was too late.

10   The father watched in horror as his son fell into the water. He flew to shore to try to save his son, but he found nothing except a few seagull feathers floating in the ocean.

5. What is a lesson that readers can learn from the myth "The Story of Icarus?"

_____
_____
_____
_____

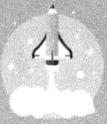

6. Which detail from the passage helps to convey the lesson in this myth?
    A. "As Icarus became a teenager, he began to want a life of his own outside of the cave."
    B. "As the father and son started to fly, Icarus loved the freedom he felt."
    C. "But Icarus didn't listen. As he flew even higher, he began to feel the wax melting down his arms."
    D. "For many days, the father and son collected seagull feathers."

7. Why are the father and Icarus imprisoned?
    A. They committed a crime.
    B. The King wanted Icarus' father to make inventions only for him.
    C. Icarus is dangerous.
    D. The King is evil and dislikes Icarus' father.

8. What would be another good title for this myth?
    A. The Greedy King
    B. Flying
    C. The Inventor and His Inventions
    D. The Disobedient Son

READING: LITERATURE

DESCRIBE CHARACTERS & EXPLAIN THEIR ACTIONS

RL.1.3 Describe characters in a story (e.g., their traits, motivations, or feelings) and explain how their actions contribute to the sequence of events.

Directions: Read the passage and answer the questions that follow.

Passage 1: The Camping Trip

1   All week long, Jessica and her friend Tia had been planning their first camping trip. It wasn't technically a real camping trip, since it would be in Tia's backyard, but they were determined to make it as close to camping in the woods as possible.

2   The girls planned to make smores, tell ghost stories, and look at the stars.

3   The day of the camp out finally arrived, and it was all Jessica and Tia could talk about at school. Later that night, the girls set up their sleeping bags in Tia's backyard. They made a pretend tent by throwing a sheet over some tree branches.

4   First, the girls decided to make smores. "You brought the marshmallows, right Jessica?" asked Tia.

5   "Oh no!" said Jessica. "I forgot the marshmallows!"

6   Tia didn't want to make Jessica feel bad, so she said, "That's okay. We can just eat chocolate and graham crackers!" It wasn't the same, but the girls pretended they were eating real smores.

7   Next, they decided to look at the stars. But the sky was dark and overcast, and there were no stars to be seen.

8   "Well, let's try telling ghost stories," said Tia. The girls started telling spooky stories, and they were having a great time. Then, suddenly, big drops of rain started pouring down.

9   The girls ran inside. Instead of feeling disappointed, they started planning an even better camping trip for another day.

1. Many problems happen on Tia and Jessica's camp out. What do Tia and Jessica's reactions to these problems tell you about them?
    A. They don't like camping very much.
    B. They both have positive attitudes.
    C. They will probably never try to camp again.
    D. They have a good sense of humor.

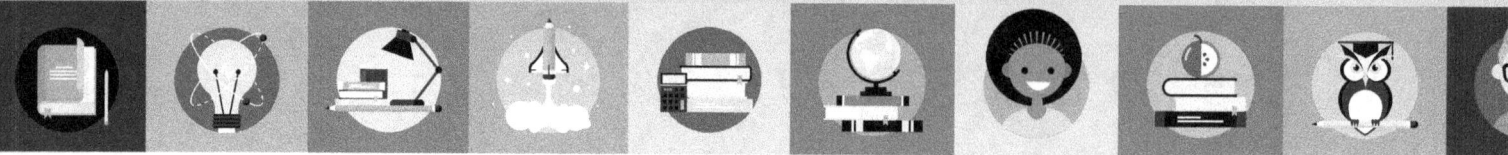

2. When Jessica forgets the marshmallows, Tia says, "That's okay. We can just eat chocolate and graham crackers!" What does this tell you about Tia as a character?
   A. She's a good friend.
   B. She doesn't like marshmallows.
   C. She's selfish.
   D. She's forgetful.

3. Would you like to be friends with Jessica and Tia? Use details from the story to support your answer.

_____
_____
_____
_____
_____
_____

4. Select two details that show Tia and Jessica are flexible when things don't go the way they planned.
   ☐ "The girls planned to make smores, tell ghost stories, and look at the stars." (Paragraph 2)
   ☐ "It wasn't the same, but the girls pretended they were eating real smores." (Paragraph 6)
   ☐ "The girls started telling spooky stories, and they were having a great time." (Paragraph 8)
   ☐ "Instead of feeling disappointed, they started planning an even better camping trip for another day." (Paragraph 9)

READING: LITERATURE

Passage 2: Leaf Games

1   Lauren pouted as she dragged the rake across the fallen leaves for what felt like the hundredth time. "I'm going to be out here all day," she sighed.

2   Just then, her neighbor Drew rode by on his red bicycle. "Hey!" said Drew. "You look like you could use some help."

3   Lauren was shocked. She couldn't imagine that anyone would ever volunteer to help with such a boring task. "Are you sure?" she asked.

4   Drew got off his bike and walked over to Lauren. "Of course!" he said. "Let's do a leaf jump." Drew ran and jumped into one of the piles Lauren had raked, scattering leaves everywhere.

5   "You try!" said Drew.

6   Lauren ran and jumped into another pile. "That is pretty fun!" she said, laughing. "But we're making a big mess."

7   Drew looked around. "True," he said. "Okay, let's do a race. You use this rake and I'll use this one. We have to race across the yard while dragging the rake behind us to rake these leaves. First one to the other side wins. Got it?"

8   "Got it!" said Lauren. She and Drew started running across the yard, dragging the rakes behind them. Drew got to the other side first, but Lauren challenged him to a rematch. "It was my first try!" she explained.

9   At dinner that night, Lauren's parents told her she had done a great job raking the leaves. "That might have to be your chore from now on," said Lauren's dad.

10   Lauren smiled. "Okay!" she said. "Raking leaves isn't so bad."

5. How does Lauren's attitude about raking leaves change from the beginning of the story to the end? Use details from the passage to support your answer.

_____

_____

_____

_____

_____

6. This question has two parts. First, answer Part A. Then, answer Part B.

Part A

How is Drew in Passage 2 similar to Jessica and Tia in Passage 1?

    A. He can make the best of a bad situation.
    B. He likes the outdoors.
    C. He has a good sense of humor.
    D. He's good at playing games.

Part B

What detail from Passage 2 best supports your answer in Part A?

    A. "Just then, her neighbor Drew rode by on his red bicycle." (Paragraph 2)
    B. "Drew got off his bike and walked over to Lauren." (Paragraph 4)
    C. "'Of course!' he said. 'Let's do a leaf jump!'" (Paragraph 4)
    D. "'You try!' said Drew." (Paragraph 5)

7. Do you think that Drew is a good friend? Use details from the passage to support your response.

_____

_____

_____

8. How do Lauren and Drew's feelings about raking leaves at the beginning of the passage differ? Use details from the passage to support your answer.

Lauren:

_____

Supporting Detail:

_____

_____

_____

Drew:

_____

Supporting Detail:

_____

_____

_____

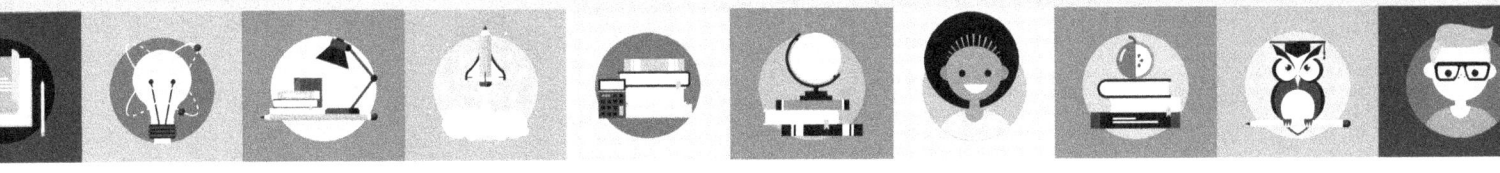

DETERMINE WORD MEANING IN CONTEXT

RL.2.4 Determine the meaning of words and phrases as they are used in a text, distinguishing literal from nonliteral language.

Directions: Answer the questions below.

It was the day of the school spelling bee, and I was sitting on the stage waiting for my turn. My palms were sweating, and **my heart was beating like a drum.** I had practiced for weeks, but I worried that I would suddenly forget all of the words I had studied.

1. Determine the meaning of the bolded phrase above.
   - **A.** The author is very excited.
   - **B.** The author is feeling sick.
   - **C.** The author isn't prepared for the spelling bee.
   - **D.** The author is nervous.

2. Josie was so sleepy and bored that she **dozed off** right there on the couch.
   What is the meaning of the bolded phrase above?

   _____
   _____

3. Benny was very careful as he walked across the old bridge. He knew that if he made one wrong move, he would **plunge** straight down into the water below.
   What detail(s) in the text above helps the reader know the meaning of the word **plunge?**

   _____
   _____

4. We all have challenges in life. We all have our mountains to climb. For me, it's math class. Math isn't easy for me. But I know if I work hard and keep trying, I'll make it to the top one day.
   What does the author compare his struggles in math class to?

   _____
   _____

READING: LITERATURE

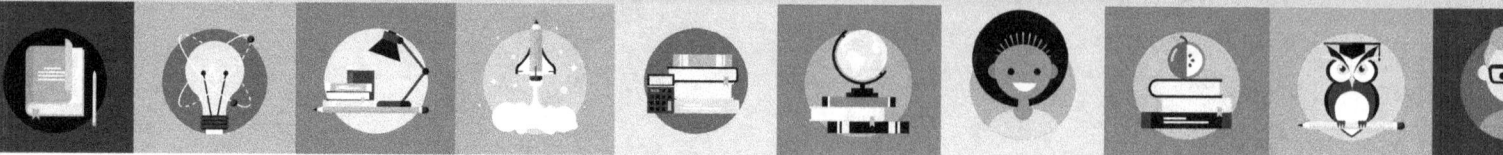

5. Liz was so **swift** that she won every race at school, and it was never even close.
   What does the word **swift** mean in the above sentence?
   - **A.** Fast
   - **B.** Athletic
   - **C.** Clever
   - **D.** Brave

6. After we kicked the soccer ball into Old Man Frank's yard, almost everyone was too scared to go and get it. But not Peter. He walked right into the mean man's yard. Peter had **nerves of steel.**
   What does the phrase **nerves of steel** mean in the sentence above?
   - **A.** Determination
   - **B.** Patience
   - **C.** Courage
   - **D.** Kindness

7. Peter walked into the backyard, and we couldn't see him anymore. We anxiously looked at one another, worried about what would happen next. We all **caught our breath** and listened for the sound of Old Man Frank yelling. At first, we didn't hear anything.
   What detail in the text above helps the reader know what the phrase **caught our breath** means?
   - **A.** "Peter walked into the backyard…"
   - **B.** "…and listened for the sound of Old Man Frank yelling."
   - **C.** "…and we couldn't see him anymore."
   - **D.** "…worried about what would happen next."

8. But soon, we heard it: Old Man Frank. Except he wasn't yelling. He was just talking to Peter, asking him questions like, "How often do you boys play soccer?" He even told Peter a story about when he played soccer as a young boy. Maybe all of our **assumptions** about Old Man Frank had been wrong. It seemed like he wasn't so scary after all.
   What are two details in the text above that help you to understand the meaning of the word **assumptions**?

   _____
   _____
   _____
   _____

22 READING: LITERATURE

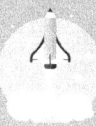

IDENTIFY & UNDERSTAND PARTS OF TEXTS

RL.2.5 Refer to parts of stories, dramas, and poems when writing or speaking about a text, using terms such as chapter, scene, and stanza; describe how each successive part builds on earlier sections.

Directions: Answer the questions below.

1. A paragraph is to a story like a stanza is to _____.
   - **A.** A topic
   - **B.** A poem
   - **C.** An illustration
   - **D.** Words

2. A paragraph is to a story like a _____ is to a play.
   - **A.** Stanza
   - **B.** Scene
   - **C.** Character
   - **D.** Text Feature

3. What is the main purpose of line breaks in a poem?
   - **A.** To organize the poem into chapters.
   - **B.** To help the reader read with emotion.
   - **C.** To enhance ideas and meaning.
   - **D.** To let the reader take a breath.

4. When does the author usually introduce the characters and describe the setting in a story? Explain why.

   _____
   _____
   _____
   _____

5. When is a story's problem usually solved? Explain why.

   _____
   _____
   _____

READING: LITERATURE

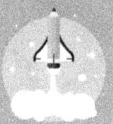

The Sheep
Ann and Jane Taylor

Directions: Read the poem and answer the questions that follow.

1. "Lazy sheep, pray tell me why
   In the pleasant fields you lie,
   Eating grass, and daisies white,
   From the morning till the night?
   Everything can something do,
   But what kind of use are you?"

2. "Nay, my little master, nay,
   Do not serve me so, I pray;
   Don't you see the wool that grows
   On my back, to make you clothes?
   Cold, and very cold, you'd be
   If you had not wool from me.

3. True, it seems a pleasant thing,
   To nip the daisies in the spring;
   But many chilly nights I pass
   On the cold and dewy grass,
   Or pick a scanty dinner, where
   All the common's brown and bare.

4. Then the farmer comes at last,
   When the merry spring is past,
   And cuts my woolly coat away,
   To warm you in the winter's day:
   Little master, this is why
   In the pleasant fields I lie."

6. How many stanzas does this poem have?
   - **A.** 5
   - **B.** 4
   - **C.** 10
   - **D.** 16

7. Which lines describe best why the master should appreciate the sheep?
    A. True, it seems a pleasant thing,
       To nip the daisies in the spring;

    B. But many chilly nights I pass
       On the cold and dewy grass,

    C. Don't you see the wool that grows
       On my back, to make you clothes?

    D. Everything can something do,
       But what kind of use are you?"

8. Read these lines from the poem:

    Then the farmer comes at last,
    When the merry spring is past,
    And cuts my woolly coat away,
    To warm you in the winter's day:

    Why do you think the author included this information?
    A. To help readers imagine how a woolly coat can keep them warm.
    B. To show that the main benefit of owning a sheep comes in winter, not spring.
    C. To show that winter will soon arrive.
    D. To suggest that the farmer would like a woolly coat.

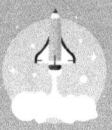

IDENTIFY POINT OF VIEW OF SELF & AUTHOR/CHARACTERS

RL.2.6 Student should be able to distinguish own point of view from that of the narrator or those of the characters.

Directions: Answer the questions below.

1. What is a story's point of view?
    - **A.** How the characters are introduced.
    - **B.** The story's lesson or moral.
    - **C.** Who is narrating or telling the story.
    - **D.** The problem that must be solved in the story.

2. What is a third-person point of view?
    - **A.** When a character in the story is the narrator and uses words like I, me, and we.
    - **B.** When the narrator is not part of the story and uses words like he, she, and they.
    - **C.** When there is only one character in the story.
    - **D.** When the main character is the first person mentioned in the story.

Directions: Read the passage below and answer the questions.

Home at Last

1   It was cold and rainy outside, but I had nowhere to go. I hid under some bushes to try to shield myself from the rain.

2   Later, I tried to run across the street to find better shelter. Drivers honked angrily as their cars almost hit me. "Get out of the way!" someone yelled.

3   The rain was slowing down, but now I was hungry. I walked around looking for food. Someone threw a bread crust on the sidewalk, so I ran over to eat it. "Get lost!" a man yelled as I walked across his path.

4   But then another man saw me and bent down, smiling. "Hi, little puppy," he said. "Aren't you cute?"

5   It was the first time someone had been nice to me in days. I wagged my tail happily.

6   "Are you lost?" he asked. "Do you have anywhere to go?"

7   I wanted to explain to the man that I didn't have a home, but he seemed to understand anyway. "Do you want to come home with me?" he asked.

8   I wagged my tail again. The man picked me up, put me in his car, and drove me to his house.

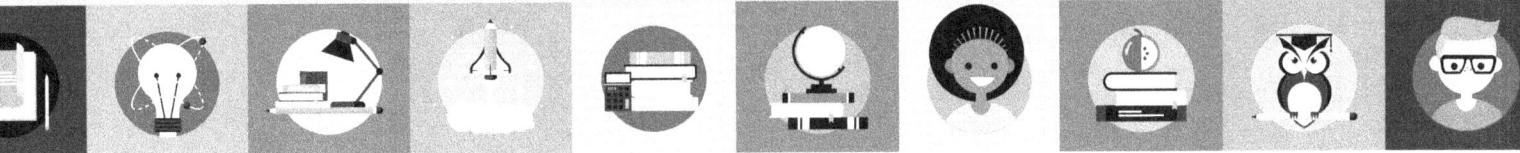

9   "A dog?" asked his wife. "Are you crazy? We don't need a dog."

10   I was scared that I would have to go back outside, but the man asked his wife, "Please, Susie?" The woman agreed, but she didn't look very happy.

3. This question has two parts. First, answer Part A. Then, answer Part B.

Part A
Who is the narrator of this story?
- **A.** A man
- **B.** A woman
- **C.** A puppy
- **D.** A young boy

Part B
What character in the story gives the reader insight as to the narrator's identity?
- **A.** The man who yells, "Get out of the way!"
- **B.** The man who brings the puppy home.
- **C.** The woman
- **D.** The rain

4. From what point of view is this story written?
   - **A.** First person
   - **B.** Second person
   - **C.** Third person
   - **D.** Fourth person

5. What does the author do to make you feel bad for the puppy? Use details from the passage to support your answer.

_____

_____

_____

_____

6. What is the feeling of the narrator at the beginning of this story?
   - **A.** Happy
   - **B.** Bored
   - **C.** Cold
   - **D.** Tired

READING: LITERATURE

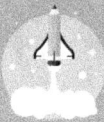

7. This question has two parts. First, answer Part A. Then, answer Part B.

Part A

What detail in the story best shows the woman's point of view about the dog?

    A. "The woman agreed..."
    B. "...but she didn't look very happy."
    C. "I was scared that I would have to go back outside."
    D. "The man asked his wife, 'Please, Susie?'"

Part B

What information about the dog might change the woman's point of view?

    A. The dog is homeless.
    B. The dog needs a bath.
    C. The dog has fleas.
    D. The dog is scared of humans.

8. How do the other human characters in the story have a different point of view than the man who takes the dog home? Use details from the story to support your response.

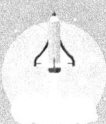

IDENTIFY HOW ILLUSTRATIONS CONVEY INFORMATION

RL.3.7 Explain how specific aspects of a text's illustrations contribute to what is conveyed by the words in a story (e.g., create mood, emphasize aspects of a character or setting).

Directions: Read the text and observe the images below, then answer the questions.

Passage 1: The First Day of School

Nathan and Julie were twins and best friends. They never got to be in the same class, but third grade was different. This year, Nathan and Julie had the same teacher!

The twins had just gotten home from the first day of third grade, and all they could talk about was how nice their new teacher seemed. Most of their best friends were also in the same class.

Some of the topics they would be learning about seemed a little challenging, but Nathan and Julie were confident that third grade would be a good year.

1. What do you think is happening in this picture? Why?

_____

_____

_____

2. How do the characters (Nathan and Julie) feel in this picture? Why do you think so? Use evidence from both the text and the pictures to support your response.

_____

_____

_____

READING: LITERATURE

3. What clues does the author give you to show you that Nathan and Julie are confident that third grade will be a great year? Use at least one piece of evidence from both the text and the pictures to support your response.

_____
_____
_____
_____

Passage 2: My Giant Dog

I have the friendliest, sweetest dog in the world. He's also enormous. My dog is so big that a lot of people think he's scary or mean.

But his heart is just as big as the rest of him. Whenever I'm feeling sad, he notices and comes to cuddle with me. He walks my little brother and me to the school bus every morning to make sure we're safe. When we get home from school, he greets us enthusiastically, wagging his tail and trying to lick us. I can't imagine a better dog. My older sister even taught him to dance!

From my giant dog, I've learned not to judge others based on their appearance. My dog may be a giant, but he's not mean or scary.

4. What physical characteristic about the dog does this image emphasize?
    A. The dog is hungry
    B. The dog is enormous.
    C. The dog is cute.
    D. The dog is funny.

5. What character trait of the dog's does this image emphasize?
    A. He's mean.
    B. He's scary and intimidating.
    C. He's scared.
    D. He's sweet and loving.

6. What is the purpose of the image above? How does it add to the information in the text?

_____
_____
_____

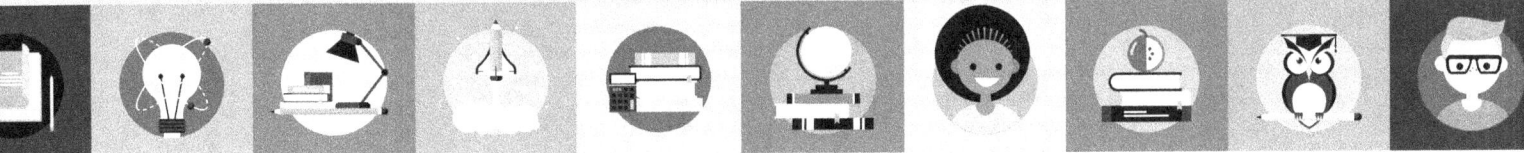

7. Look at the image below.

How do you think the boy is feeling in the picture above? Explain why.

_____
_____
_____
_____
_____
_____
_____

   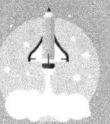      

COMPARE & CONTRAST NARRATIVES

RL.3.9 Compare and contrast the themes, settings, and plots of stories written by the same author about the same or similar characters (e.g., in books from a series).

Directions: Read the passages below and answer the questions.

Passage 1: The Goose and the Golden Egg
Adapted from the fable by Aesop

1   There was once a farmer who owned a golden goose. Every day, the goose laid a beautiful, shiny golden egg.

2   People came from far and wide to see the magnificent goose and her golden eggs. The farmer began taking the eggs to market, and people would pay large amounts of money to buy them.

3   The farmer was getting richer than he had ever imagined. But he wanted more. The goose only gave the farmer one egg each day, and the farmer decided this was not enough. He became impatient with the goose.

4   One day, the farmer was counting his money when an idea came to him. If he cut the goose open, he could get all of the golden eggs at once. That way, he wouldn't have to wait for one egg each day, and he could make much more money.

5   Imagining what he would do with his riches, the farmer cut the goose. To his disappointment, he didn't find even one golden egg inside. His plan had failed!

6   And now the farmer's precious golden goose was dead. He would never lay another golden egg.

Passage 2: The Dog and His Reflection
Adapted from the fable by Aesop

1   One day, a dog was running past the butcher's shop. The butcher threw the dog a bone. The excited dog began hurrying home with his delicious prize.

2   As the dog was crossing a bridge, he looked down and saw his reflection in the water. But the dog didn't realize that he was looking at his reflection. Instead, he

thought he was looking at another dog. And he thought the other dog had a much bigger bone in his mouth!

3   If the dog had stopped to think for a minute, he might have realized his mistake. But instead of thinking, he dropped his bone and jumped at the dog in the river. He was hoping to take the bigger bone for himself.

4   Instead of getting a bone, the dog found himself having to swim frantically to shore. He finally reached the shore and dragged himself out of the water.

5   Now instead of having a bigger bone, the dog had no bone at all. He stood on the shore, thinking sadly about the delicious bone he had lost.

1. How are the farmer and the dog alike in these two stories? Use details from the passages to support your response.

_____
_____
_____
_____
_____
_____
_____

2. This question has two parts. First, answer Part A. Then, answer Part B.

Part A
What is the setting of the first passage?
   A. A river
   B. A farm
   C. A mountain
   D. A school

Part B
What is the setting of the second passage?
   A. A river
   B. A farm
   C. A mountain
   D. A school

3. This question has two parts. First, answer Part A. Then, answer Part B.

Part A

Which of the following could be a theme of both stories?

    A. Make good choices.

    B. Be careful who you trust.

    C. Treat others the way that you want to be treated.

    D. Be grateful for what you have instead of being greedy.

Part B

What detail from the first passage helps develop this theme?

    A. "People came from far and wide to see the magnificent goose and her golden eggs." (Paragraph 2)

    B. "The farmer was getting richer than he had ever imagined." (Paragraph 3)

    C. "The farmer was counting his money when an idea came to him." (Paragraph 4)

    D. "And now the farmer's precious golden goose was dead. He would never lay another golden egg." (Paragraph 6)

4. What decision do the characters make in Passage 1 and in Passage 2, and what are the results?

The farmer's decision:

_____
_____

The result:

_____
_____
_____

The dog's decision:

_____
_____

The result:

_____
_____

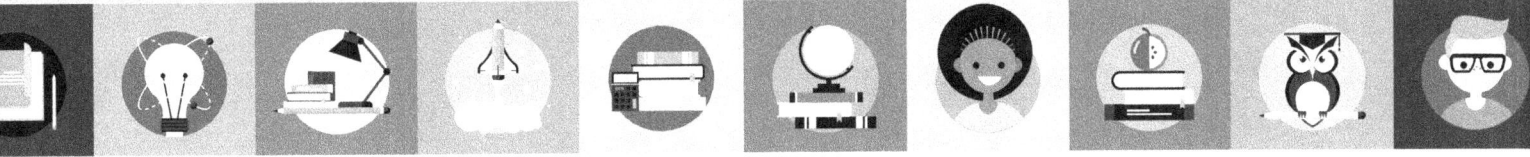

5. What is the problem in both stories?
    A. The main characters want more than what they have.
    B. Other characters try to take what the main characters have.
    C. The main characters both get lost.
    D. The main characters don't have enough money to buy something important.

6. What caused the farmer to cut open his goose? Use details from the story to support your answer.

_____
_____
_____
_____

7. Why did the dog jump into the river? Use details from the story to support your answer.

_____
_____
_____
_____

8. Select the sentences below that show how the farmer and the dog are different
    ☐ The farmer wants more money, while the dog wants a bigger bone.
    ☐ The farmer mistakenly thinks he can get more eggs if he cuts open the goose, while the dog mistakenly thinks his reflection is another dog with a bigger bone.
    ☐ The dog loses his bone and the farmer accidentally kills his goose.
    ☐ A farmer gave the dog a bone, while the farmer gets his golden goose from the market
    ☐ The dog's story takes place on a river, while the farmer's story takes place on a farm.
    ☐ The farmer is happy at the end of the story, while the dog is scared at the end of the story.

READING: LITERATURE

READING: INFORMATION

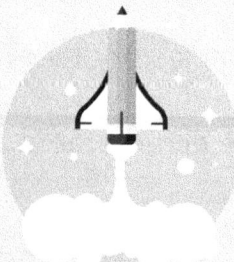

ASK & ANSWER QUESTIONS USING TEXT EVIDENCE

RI.1.1 Ask and answer questions to demonstrate understanding of a text, referring explicitly to the text as the basis for the answers.

Directions: Read the passage and answer the questions that follow.

Passage 1: About the Starfish

1   Marine scientists are trying to change the name "starfish" to "sea star" because the name isn't accurate. Why? The starfish is not a fish.

2   Like fish, the starfish does live underwater. However, it doesn't have scales, gills, or fins. It can only live in saltwater. The starfish is actually an echinoderm, like sand dollars and sea urchins.

3   Around the world, there are about 2,000 different species of starfish. Most of them have five arms, but some have 10 arms, 20 arms, or even 40 arms. They have hard, bony skin that can protect them from predators. Most of them also have bright colors that can scare off predators or be used as camouflage to hide from predators.

4   Starfish, or sea stars, are very unique animals. They have one eye on the tip of each arm, and their eyes can't see color. They don't have brains or blood. Instead of blood, starfish have sea water running through their bodies.

5   If a starfish loses an arm, they have the amazing ability to make it grow back. Some species can even grow a whole new sea star from a broken arm.

1. The name "starfish" is not accurate because the starfish
    - **A.** does not look like a star.
    - **B.** is not a fish.
    - **C.** doesn't live underwater.
    - **D.** has scales, but not fins or gills.

2. Which of the following is NOT a way that starfish protect themselves from predators?
    - **A.** Their skin is hard and bony.
    - **B.** They use their bright colors to scare predators.
    - **C.** They have sharp spikes on each arm.
    - **D.** They also use their bright colors as camouflage to hide from predators.

   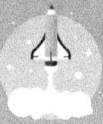     

3. List three things that make the starfish a unique animal.

   1. _____

   2. _____

   3. _____

4. How many arms does the starfish have? Use evidence from the text to support your answer.

_____
_____
_____
_____
_____
_____

Passage 2: The Starfish Killer

1   Back in 2012, millions of starfish started dying out across North America. A mysterious starfish killer turned these sea stars into piles of "white goo" or "white slime."

2   Recently, scientists have discovered exactly what has been killing starfish. It's a type of parvovirus. The virus causes starfish to become weak, and it leaves them open to bacterial infections. The bacterial infection kills the sea star.

3   About 8-17 days after infection, the starfish starts to develop white sores on its body. Sometimes, the starfish's arms rip off and walk away. Eventually, the starfish melts into a pile of white goo.

4   This virus isn't new, but scientists aren't sure what's causing it to kill so many starfish. In the past, the virus only attacked one or two species at a time. Now, over 20 species of starfish have been affected, including the sunflower star, the giant pink star, and the rainbow star.

5   Some scientists think the virus is spreading so quickly because there are so many sea stars packed into small areas.

6   Scientists are continuing to study this parvovirus to see if they can stop it. If they can't stop it, scientists hope to be able to prevent it from happening again in the future.

5. Using details from the passage, complete the sequence of events below.

   (1) The starfish catches the parvovirus.

   (2) _____

   (3) The starfish gets a bacterial infection.

   (4) _____

   (5) _____

   (6) The starfish melts into a pile of white goo.

6. Where is the parvovirus mostly killing starfish?
   A. North America
   B. Around the world
   C. Asia
   D. The Caribbean

7. The following question has two parts. First, answer Part A. Then, answer Part B.

Part A

The parvovirus isn't new. But what is different about the virus nowadays?

    A. It's affecting starfish all over the world.

    B. It's affecting many different species of starfish.

    C. It's turning starfish to white goo.

    D. It's killing starfish in days instead of weeks.

Part B

What do scientists think the reason is for the change in Part A?

    A. The virus is growing more powerful.

    B. Starfish aren't as strong as they were in the past.

    C. There are large numbers of starfish packed into small areas.

    D. This is a different type of parvovirus.

8. Based on the details in the passage, what inference can be made about how scientists will respond to the parvovirus? Use details from the passage to support your answer.

_____

_____

_____

_____

_____

_____

_____

_____

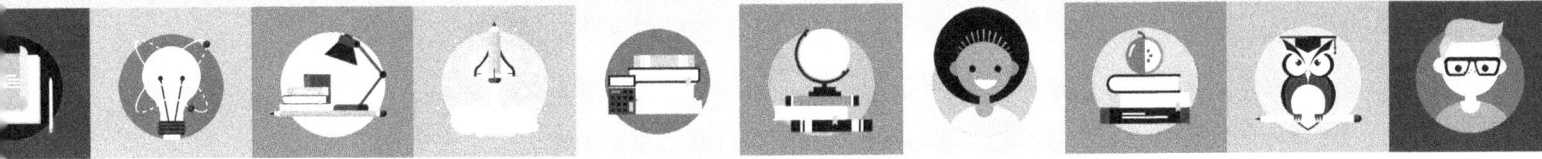

DETERMINE MAIN IDEA & EXPLAIN KEY DETAILS

RI.1.2 Determine the main idea of a text; recount the key details and explain how they support the main idea.

Directions: Read the passage and answer the questions that follow.

Passage 1: The Invention of the Potato Chip

1   Have you ever eaten a potato chip and wondered how this salty treat was invented? Maybe through lots of time, effort, and experimenting?

2   Actually, the answer might surprise you. The potato chip was invented completely by accident. A hotel chef named George Crum cooked some fried potatoes for his customers. But the customers thought George's fried potatoes were disgusting. They complained that the potatoes were too thick and too bland, or flavorless.

3   George Crum was furious that the customers had complained about his food. He decided to teach them a lesson. George grabbed some more potatoes and sliced them until they were as thin as a piece of paper. Next, he put an excessive amount of salt on them.

4   George was sure that the customers would think that these fried potatoes were even worse, and they would learn to appreciate his delicious food.

5   Instead, the customers loved the new fried potatoes! Soon, everyone was talking about the tasty potato chips that George Crum had invented.

6   So next time you eat a bag of potato chips, remember that it all started with a hotel chef trying to prank his rude customers.

1. Select the statement that describes the main idea of the article.
    A. George Crum was not a very nice chef.
    B. Potato chips were invented by accident.
    C. Customers should be polite, not rude.
    D. Sometimes our plans don't go the way we expect.

2. List at least two details that support the main idea.

_____

_____

_____

3. Which quote from the passage best supports the main idea?

A. "George Crum was furious that the customers had complained about his food." (Paragraph 3)

B. "They complained that the potatoes were too thick and too bland, or flavorless." (Paragraph 2)

C. "So next time you eat a bag of potato chips, remember that it all started with a hotel chef trying to prank his customers." (Paragraph 6)

D. "Instead, the customers loved the new fried potatoes!" (Paragraph 5)

4. What is another title that could be used for this passage?

A. The Rude Customers
B. The Angry Chef
C. Hotel Cooking Adventures
D. Potato Chips: A Happy Accident

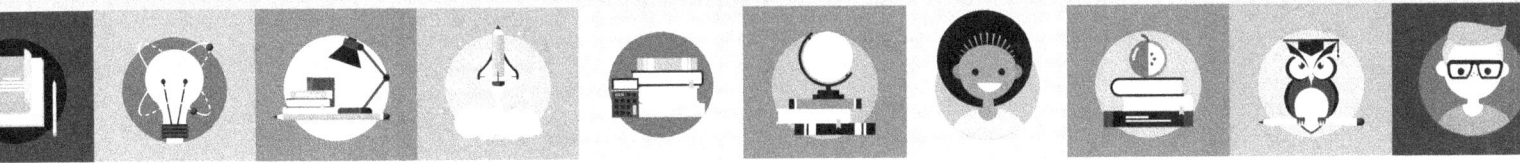

Passage 2: The Invention of Baseball

1   Until 2011, popular legend was that a man named Abner Doubleday invented the sport of baseball. Abner Doubleday was a man who eventually fired one of the first shots in the Civil War, and he became a heroic general.

2   According to the legend, 20-year-old Doubleday invented the sport in 1939 in Cooperstown, New York. He used a stick to draw his idea for baseball in the dirt. It was a new game he had invented that he and his friends could play.

3   The story was so popular that the National Baseball Hall of Fame was opened in Cooperstown, New York, where baseball was supposedly invented.

4   But the truth is that Doubleday did not invent baseball. Major League Baseball's historian, John Thorn, published a book explaining that baseball was played long before 1939. As early as the 1800's, different versions of baseball were played in New York, Philadelphia, and Massachusetts. A similar bat and ball game, called Rounders, was also played in Britain.

5   So who did invent baseball? Historian John Thorn says that this is one question that will probably never be answered.

5. Which of the following best describes the main idea of this passage?
   A. Despite the popular legend that Abner Doubleday invented baseball, we don't know who actually invented the sport.
   B. Different versions of baseball were played in New York, Philadelphia, Massachusetts, and even Britain.
   C. According to legend, 20-year-old Abner Doubleday invented the sport of baseball in Cooperstown, New York in 1939.
   D. John Thorn published a book explaining that Abner Doubleday did not invent baseball, because baseball was being played long before 1939.

6. List at least two details that support or develop the main idea.

   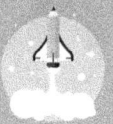      

7. Which of the following quotes does NOT support the main idea of this passage?
   A. "As early as the 1800's, different versions of baseball were played in New York, Philadelphia, and Massachusetts." (Paragraph 4)
   B. "The story was so popular that the National Baseball Hall of Fame was opened in Cooperstown, New York, where baseball was supposedly invented." (Paragraph 3)
   C. "But the truth is that Doubleday did not invent baseball." (Paragraph 4)
   D. "Abner Doubleday was a man who eventually fired one of the first shots in the Civil War, and he became a heroic general." (Paragraph 1)

8. Who invented baseball?
   A. Abner Doubleday
   B. John Thorn
   C. We'll probably never know.
   D. Someone in Britain who called the game "Rounders."

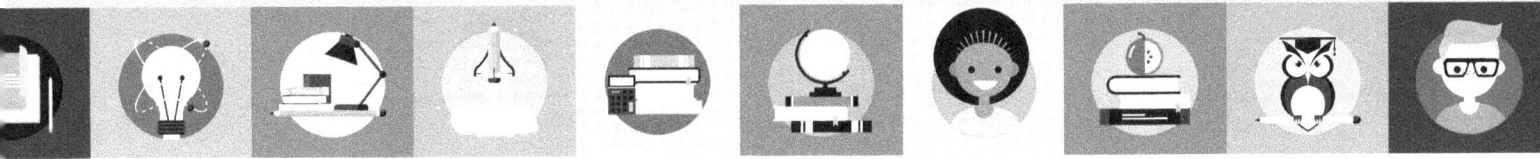

DESCRIBE & UNDERSTAND RELATIONSHIPS BETWEEN IDEAS

RI.3.3 Describe the relationship between a series of historical events, scientific ideas or concepts, or steps in technical procedures in a text, using language that pertains to time, sequence, and cause/effect.

Directions: Read the passage and answer the questions that follow.

Passage 1: The Sinking of The Titanic

1   On April 15, 1912, a huge steamship called the Titanic hit an iceberg and sank to the bottom of the Atlantic Ocean. Over 1,500 people drowned in the tragic accident. It was the very first time the Titanic had sailed.

2   At the time, the Titanic was the largest ship that had ever been built. It had a swimming pool, a gym, several cafes, a library, a barber shop, and more. People believed it was "the safest ship ever."

3   Because people thought the ship was unsinkable, there were only 20 lifeboats on board. This was enough to hold only half of the passengers and crew. Nothing bad could happen to the Titanic, people thought. But when something bad did happen, there weren't enough lifeboats to get everyone to safety.

4   The Titanic also received at least five warnings that there was ice ahead, but the warnings were ignored. Some historians say that the captain, Edward J. Smith, was trying to cross the Atlantic faster than another ship, the Olympic. For an icy area, the Titanic was traveling way too fast.

5   If the ship had been moving slower, they might have seen the iceberg in time. The ship also might have hit the iceberg with less force and caused less damage.

1. Why were there only 20 lifeboats on board the Titanic?
    A. 20 was the correct number of lifeboats for a ship that size.
    B. People thought that the Titanic was unsinkable.
    C. It was too expensive to buy more lifeboats.
    D. 20 lifeboats would hold all of the passengers and crew.

2. Why do many historians believes the Titanic was traveling so fast?
    A. The captain wanted to beat the speed of another ship.
    B. They were trying to get away from the icebergs.
    C. There was a storm coming, and the captain wanted to beat it.
    D. The Titanic was traveling the appropriate speed.

READING: INFORMATION   45

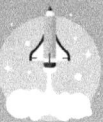

3. What are two factors that made the Titanic accident worse? Use evidence from the text to support your response.

_____
_____
_____
_____
_____
_____
_____

4. How did people's beliefs about the Titanic affect what happened to the ship? Use details from the text to support your answer.

_____
_____
_____
_____
_____
_____
_____

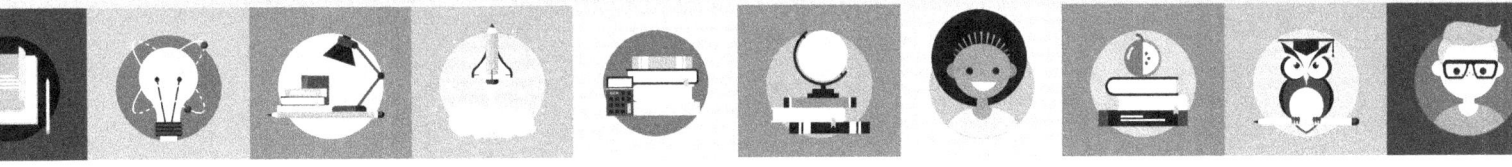

Passage 2: The Great Chicago Fire

1   In 1871, almost the entire city of Chicago was made of wood. There were wooden buildings, wooden sidewalks, and even wooden streets. Therefore, it's no surprise that the Great Chicago Fire of October 8, 1871 spread quickly and caused major damage.

2   The week before the Great Chicago Fire, there were 20 fires in the city. The firefighters were exhausted when they got a call on October 8th around 9:00 PM that a fire had started behind the O'Leary home. Catherine and Patrick O'Leary lived in the home with their five children.

3   At first, the firefighters were sent to the wrong neighborhood. By the time they finally got to the O'Leary house, the fire was out of control. The fire continued to burn for two days until rain fell and extinguished it. Thousands of buildings burnt down, and hundreds of people died in the fire.

4   Mrs. O'Leary explained to reporters that she was sleeping when the fire started. But newspapers reported that she was milking her cow in the barn and the cow kicked over a lantern, starting the terrible fire. Almost everyone in Chicago blamed Mrs. O'Leary for the destructive fire. After the fire, everyone was so angry with Mrs. O'Leary that she stayed in her house and avoided other people.

5   Architects rebuilt Chicago with the world's first skyscrapers. The population and the economy grew, and Chicago became a great city again.

5. List at least two reasons that the Great Chicago Fire spread so quickly.

_____
_____
_____
_____
_____

6. Why was the fire out of control by the time the firefighters got to the O'Leary house?
   A. Mrs. O'Leary was sleeping when the fire started.
   B. Mrs. O'Leary's cow had kicked over the lantern.
   C. The firefighters were sent to the wrong neighborhood first.
   D. The firefighters were sleeping and took too long to get to the house.

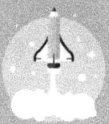

7. Who or what did the people of Chicago blame for the fire?
    A. The wooden buildings, sidewalks, and streets
    B. Mrs. O'Leary and her cow
    C. The exhausted firefighters who went to the wrong neighborhood
    D. Mrs. O'Leary's five children

8. What was one positive effect of the Chicago Fire? Use details from the passage to support your response.

    _____
    _____
    _____
    _____

9. How did the Chicago Fire change Mrs. O'Leary's life? Use details from the passage to support your answer.

    _____
    _____
    _____
    _____
    _____

10. What finally stopped The Great Chicago Fire?
    A. The Chicago firefighters
    B. The rain
    C. A team of volunteers
    D. Firefighters from neighboring cities

11. How are Passage 1 (The Sinking of the Titanic) and Passage 2 (The Great Chicago Fire) similar? Be sure to use at least 1 detail from each passage to support your answer.

    _____
    _____
    _____
    _____
    _____
    _____

DETERMINE DOMAIN-SPECIFIC WORD MEANING IN CONTEXT

RI.2.4 Determine the meaning of general academic and domain-specific words and phrases in a text relevant to a grade 3 topic or subject area.

Directions: Read the passage and answer the questions that follow.

Passage 1: The Cactus Plant

1   The cactus is a type of plant known as a succulent. It can store water to drink later if it doesn't rain for a long time. Cacti (more than one cactus plant) can store water in their stems, roots, and leaves. In fact, a cactus plant can live for an entire year without rain.

2   How does the cactus plant store so much water? Its spikes, which are actually called spines, help prevent the water from escaping. The cactus plant's waxy skin helps it hold in water too.

3   When you envision a cactus plant, you probably picture a spiky green plant. Actually, there are about 2,000 different types of cacti. Most are green, but some have a bluish or brownish hue. Some are flat and some are round, and they come in many unique shapes. They also grow large flowers that can be yellow, red, pink, white, orange, or blue. Some cacti even grow fruit.

4   Cacti do grow mostly in the desert or in other dry areas because they require dry, rocky soil. However, some cacti have been found in rainforests or as far north as Canada.

5   Cactus plants are most prevalent in Arizona, California, and Texas. People visit from all over just to see the many cacti that grow in these states, especially when the flowers are blooming between the months of March and May.

1. What is the meaning of the underlined word as it is used in this sentence from the passage?

    Cactus plants are most <u>prevalent</u> in Arizona, California, and Texas. (Paragraph 5)
    - **A.** common
    - **B.** beautiful
    - **C.** large
    - **D.** opular

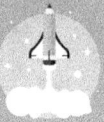

2. What is a succulent? Use details from the passage to support your answer.

   _____
   _____
   _____
   _____
   _____
   _____

3. What is the meaning of the underlined word as it is used in this sentence from the passage?

   Most are green, but some have a greenish or brownish <u>hue.</u> (Paragraph 3)
   - **A.** flower
   - **B.** color
   - **C.** fruit
   - **D.** skin

4. What is the meaning of the underlined word as it is used in this sentence from the passage?

   When you <u>envision</u> a cactus plant, you probably picture a spiky green plant. (Paragraph 3)
   - **A.** see
   - **B.** describe
   - **C.** draw
   - **D.** imagine

Passage 2: The Cocoa Bean

1   If you've ever enjoyed a chocolate bar, chocolate cake, or chocolate ice cream, then you've eaten cocoa beans. Cocoa beans grow on trees in tropical climates, and they're used to make chocolate.

2   Cocoa trees only grow close to the Equator because they need hot and somewhat wet weather to flourish. The trees also need shade to grow, so they usually grow in the shade of other plants, such as mango and papaya trees.

3   Cocoa trees produce orange fruit, called pods. The pods have seeds on the inside, and these seeds are what we call cocoa beans. The beans are a milky white color at first, and they would taste extremely bitter if you ate them right off the tree.

4   To transform these bitter cocoa beans into delicious chocolate, chocolatiers have to first dry out the beans. Once the beans are dry, they become brownish-red in color. They're then transported to a chocolate factory, where the beans are roasted.

5   The roasted cocoa beans are chopped into pieces called cocoa nibs. Heat and pressure are used to extract two liquids from the cocoa nibs: cocoa liquor and cocoa butter. These two liquids are mixed with sugar and milk powder, and we finally have the finished product!

6   The chocolate is sometimes poured into molds to give it a candy bar shape, then wrapped by a machine, and eventually placed on a shelf and purchased by kids like you. Who knew your favorite treat took such a journey to get to you?

5. What is a <u>chocolatier</u> (Paragraph 4)? Use evidence from the text to support your answer.

___

___

6. What does the author mean by the underlined phrase in this sentence from the passage?

    These two liquids are mixed with sugar and milk powder, and we finally have <u>the finished product!</u> (Paragraph 5)
    - **A.** Cocoa beans
    - **B.** Cocoa nibs
    - **C.** Chocolate
    - **D.** Candy bars

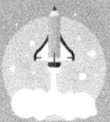

7. What is the meaning of the underlined word as it used in this sentence from the passage?

    Heat and pressure are used to <u>extract</u> two liquids from the cocoa nibs: cocoa liquor and cocoa butter. (Paragraph 5)
    - **A.** make
    - **B.** remove
    - **C.** mix
    - **D.** carry

8. Select the **TWO** correct meanings of the word <u>journey</u> as it is used in the sentence.

    Who knew your favorite chocolate bar took such a <u>journey</u> to get to you? (Paragraph 6)
    - **A.** Traveling from one place to another
    - **B.** A fun trip or vacation
    - **C.** A long process
    - **D.** Hard work
    - **E.** Ocean voyage

USE TEXT FEATURES & SEARCH TOOLS

RI.2.5 Use text features and search tools (e.g., key words, sidebars, hyperlinks) to locate information relevant to a given topic efficiently.

Directions: Read the passage and answer the questions that follow.

Passage 1: Caves

1   A cave is a space under the surface of the Earth, in cliff walls, or in hillsides. Many times, caves are a complicated system of connected underground passageways, kind of like a maze.

Types of Caves

2   Caves form over a long period of time, because the processes that make caves are very slow. There are several different processes that can make caves, and they form different types of caves.

3   **Solutional caves** are the most common, and they are formed from rainfall and chemical processes. The acid in the water eats away at the rock surface below, making a hole. The hole gets larger and larger, and eventually forms a cave.

4   Caves are also formed when hot lava from a volcano melts the rock surface below, making a hole.

5   **Sea caves** are formed when sea cliffs are eroded by waves and tides. The eroded cliff eventually forms a cave.

Cave Features

6   Rock formations decorate most caves. These formations can hang down from the ceiling, sprout up from the ground, or cover the sides of a cave.

7   The most common formations are **stalactites** and **stalagmites**. Rock formations that hang from the ceiling are called stalactites. Rock formations that sprout up from the ground are called stalagmites. Both of these are formed from dripping water.

Cave Creatures

8   Some animals like to spend time in cave entrances, but they don't live inside of caves. For example, foxes, bears, spiders, cockroaches, and frogs all like to take up shelter at cave entrances. Some birds may also build nests in cave entrances.

9   However, there are some animals that truly live in caves and these animals never go outside. Scientists who study caves, called **speleologists**, believe there are around 50,000 different species of animals that live in caves, and we will probably never discover them all.

   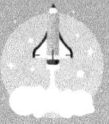      

1. What is the purpose of the headings in this passage?
   A. To tell the reader the author's opinion
   B. To help the reader visualize information
   C. To help the reader find the main idea of each section
   D. To help the reader place events in order

2. Why are some of the words in the paragraphs in bold text?
   A. To point out the main idea of the whole passage
   B. To draw the reader's attention to an important word
   C. To make the text look nice and easy to read
   D. To help the reader visualize information

3. What information can be found under the heading "Cave Features?"
   A. Caves are also formed when hot lava from a volcano melts the rock surface below.
   B. Some animals like to spend time in cave entrances but don't live in caves.
   C. Caves often hold a complicated system of connected underground passageways, kind of like a maze.
   D. Formations that hang from the ceiling are called stalactites.

4. Under which heading could the following information be added?

   "Technically, bats do not truly live in caves. This is because they sleep in caves, but they leave often to hunt for food."
   A. Cave Features
   B. Cave Creatures
   C. Types of Caves
   D. A new heading

5. Select the type text feature in the article that explains the difference between solutional caves and sea caves.
   A. Paragraphs
   B. Annotations
   C. Headings
   D. Subtitles

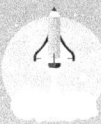

6. This question has two parts. First, answer Part A. Then, answer Part B.

Part A

What is a sea cave?

    A. A cave formed from rainfall and chemical processes.

    B. A cave formed by an erupting volcano.

    C. A rock formation formed from dripping water.

    D. A cave formed when sea cliffs are eroded by waves and tides.

Part B

Select the **TWO** text features you were able to use to find this information quickly.

    A. Footnote

    B. Headings

    C. Bold text

    D. Glossary

    E. Dictionary

7. If you wanted to search online for more information about the different types of caves, what words could you use to start your search?

    A. Solutional caves

    B. Cave features

    C. Animals that live in caves

    D. Cave Types

8. If the article included an alphabetical list of the bold words, along with their definitions, it would be called a/an:

    A. Glossary

    B. Index

    C. Hyperlink

    D. Caption

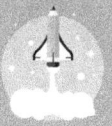

IDENTIFY POINT OF VIEW OF SELF & AUTHOR

RI.2.6 Distinguish their own point of view from that of the author of a text.

Directions: Read the passage and answer the questions that follow.

Passage 1: The Importance of Exercise

1   You probably know that exercise can make you strong and healthy, but being active might have more benefits than you realize.

2   Exercising regularly can help people maintain a healthy weight and prevent diseases like diabetes and high blood pressure. But it can also benefit your mind! Exercise produces endorphins, which are chemicals that help people feel happy and relaxed. And the more you exercise, the better your body and mind can handle situations that might make you feel stressed or anxious.

3   Exercising can also help people sleep better at night. Many people who exercise regularly feel more confident and energetic too.

4   Getting benefits from exercise doesn't require going to the gym every day or working out for hours. Just 30 minutes of physical activity can be extremely helpful. You can play a sport or a game with friends, go for a jog, ride a bike, dance, or even walk your dog. Just get up and move for 30 minutes a day, and you'll see wonderful benefits for your body and your mind.

1. Select the **TWO** sentences from the passage that best help you understand the author's point of view.
   - ☐ "Just get up and move for 30 minutes a day, and you'll see wonderful benefits for your body and mind." (Paragraph 4)
   - ☐ "Exercising can help people sleep better at night." (Paragraph 3)
   - ☐ "You probably know that exercise can make you strong and healthy, but being active might have more benefits than you realize." (Paragraph 1)
   - ☐ "You can play a sport or a game with friends, go for a job, ride a bike, dance, or even walk your dog." (Paragraph 4)

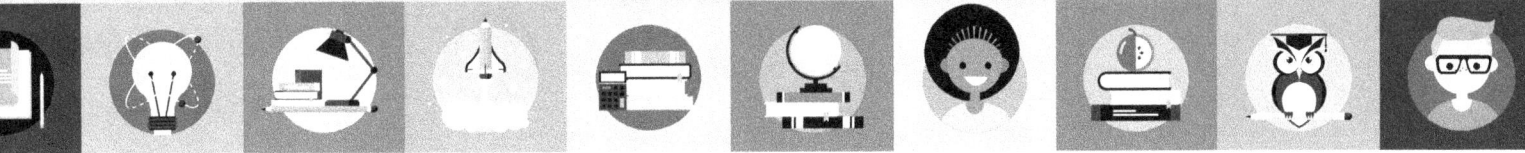

2. This question has two parts. First, answer Part A. Then, answer Part B.

Part A

Based on the information in the passage, with which statement would the author most likely agree?

    A. Eating vegetables is also extremely important.
    B. Kids should spend more time outdoors.
    C. Exercise is important for physical and mental health.
    D. Everyone should go to the gym and exercise.

Part B

Which piece of evidence from the passage supports your answer in Part A?

    A. "Exercising regularly can help people maintain a healthy weight..." (Paragraph 2)
    B. "Getting benefits from exercise doesn't require going to the gym every day or working out for hours.
    C. "You can play a sport or game with your friends, go for a job, ride a bike, dance, or even walk your dog." (Paragraph 4)
    D. "Exercising regularly can help people maintain a healthy weight and prevent diseases like diabetes and high blood pressure. But it can also benefit your mind!" (Paragraph 2)

3. Based on the information in the passage, do you agree or disagree with the author's point of view? Why? What information in the passage influenced your point of view?

READING: INFORMATION

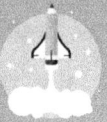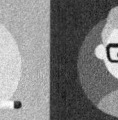

Passage 2: Turn Off the TV

1   Kids today spend plenty of time looking at screens: computer screens, phone screens, and television screens. This isn't always a bad thing, but it should be done in moderation. Too much television, for example, can harm children.

2   Kids who consistently watch more than 4 hours of TV a day are more likely to be overweight and unhealthy. Kids who see violence on TV may be more aggressive. They may also start to believe that the world is a scary place and that something bad will happen to them.

3   Today's TV shows are also filled with bad behavior that can influence children to behave badly themselves. Commercials advertise unhealthy foods and drinks that can lead to an unhealthy lifestyle.

4   Plus, too much time spent watching TV can take time away from other, healthier activities. Kids who watch too much TV may spend less time playing outside, talking to friends and family, and reading or doing homework.

5   It's okay to watch an hour or two of TV a day, but don't overdo it. It can lead to an unhealthy lifestyle, bad behavior, and less time spent on more important activities. Do yourself a favor, and turn off the TV!

4. What is the author's point of view about television?
   - **A.** It's okay to watch an hour or two of TV a day.
   - **B.** Kids who see violence on TV may be more aggressive.
   - **C.** Too much television can harm children.
   - **D.** TV commercials advertise too many unhealthy foods and drinks.

5. What are the best words to show the author's point of view about television?
   - **A.** Don't overdo it
   - **B.** 4 hours of TV a day
   - **C.** The world is a scary place
   - **D.** Do yourself a favor

6. This question has two parts. First, answer Part A. Then, answer Part B.
Part A
   Based on the information in the passage, with which statement would the author most likely agree?
   - **A.** It's best for families to not own televisions.
   - **B.** The television should be off during family dinner.
   - **C.** Activities like reading and spending time with family are healthier than watching television.
   - **D.** All kids who watch too much TV behave badly.

Part B

What piece of evidence from the passage supports your answer in Part A?

A. "Kids who consistently watch more than 4 hours of TV a day are likelier to be overweight and unhealthy." (Paragraph 2)

B. "...too much time spent watching TV can take away from other, healthier activities. Kids who spend too much time watching TV may spend less time playing outside, talking to friends and family, and reading or doing homework." (Paragraph 4)

C. "They may also start to believe that the world is a scary place and that something bad will happen to them." (Paragraph 2)

D. "Today's TV shows are also filled with bad behavior that can influence children to behave badly themselves. Commercials advertise unhealthy foods and drinks that can lead to an unhealthy lifestyle." (Paragraph 3)

7. After reading the information in this passage, do you agree or disagree with the author's point of view? Be sure to use details from the passage to support your answer.

8. How does the title of the article give you information about the author's point of view?

   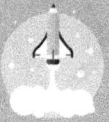      

USE & UNDERSTAND INFORMATION IN ILLUSTRATIONS

RI.3.7 Use information gained from illustrations (e.g., maps, photographs) and the words in a text to demonstrate understanding of the text (e.g., where, when, why, and how key events occur).

Directions: Read the passage and answer the questions that follow.

Passage 1: States of Matter

1   Matter is anything that takes up mass and space. In other words, matter is the "stuff" that the universe is made of. Matter is made up of atoms and molecules which combine to make up objects like the desk you're sitting in, the pencil you're holding, the paper you're reading, and even you. Matter exists in three main states (or forms): solids, liquids, and gases.

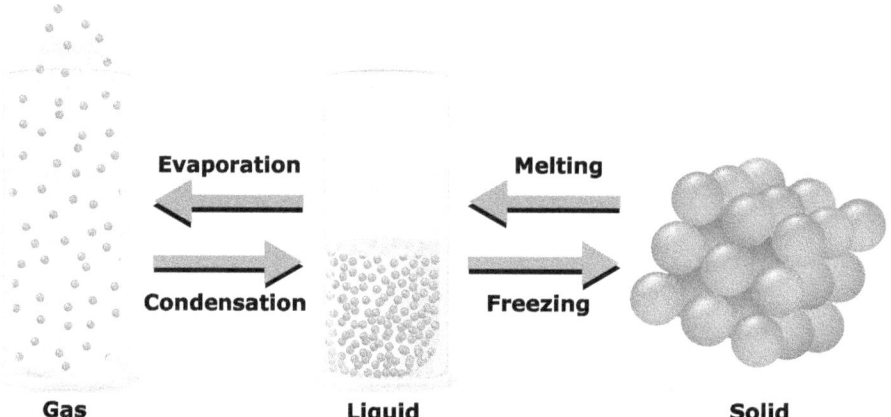

2   The air you're breathing right now is made of gases. Gas molecules are spread out and very energetic. They move around constantly. Gases are mostly invisible and have no fixed shape.

3   If you put a gas inside of a container, it will spread out to fill the whole container, no matter how big or small it is.

4   Liquids include water and soda. They are made up of molecules that aren't as spread out as gas molecules. But they're more spread out than solid molecules.

5   Liquid molecules can also move around easily, although they don't have as much energy as gas molecules. Liquids don't have their own shape. Instead, they take the shape of the container they're in.

6   Solids include you, your desk, your chair, and your friend. Solids are made up of molecules that group closely together and don't move around. Solids do have their own shape. The shape of a solid does not change when it's placed in a container.

7   Objects can sometimes change from one state of matter to another. For example, a liquid can evaporate and become a gas. A solid can melt and become a liquid, like when ice melts and turns into water. A liquid can freeze and become a solid, like when water freezes and becomes ice.

1. Based on the passage and the illustration, which state of matter has the most spread out molecules?
    A. Gas
    B. Liquid
    C. Solid
    D. None. They're all equal.

2. How does the illustration help you better understand the passage?
    A. It corrects information that was wrong in the passage.
    B. It adds information about many more states of matter.
    C. It helps readers see and imagine the information in the passage, and adds new information about the ways that states of matter change.
    D. It makes the passage more fun to read.

3. Which state of matter has its own shape that does not change?
    A. Gas
    B. Liquid
    C. Solid
    D. All of the above.

4. The passage explains that objects can change from one state of matter to another, like when melting causes a solid to become a liquid. The illustration has arrows that show how these changes can happen, including that freezing can cause a _____ to turn into a _____.

5. Based on the information in the illustration, can a liquid turn into a gas? Explain your answer.

_____

_____

6. Select the **TWO** types of molecules that move around.
    ☐ Gas
    ☐ Solid
    ☐ Liquid
    ☐ Condensation

Passage 2: Moons of the Solar System

1   Did you know that Earth isn't the only planet with a moon? In fact, some planets have moons that are bigger than Earth's moon. Jupiter, for example, has 69 moons (that we know of), and some of them are massive.

2   Jupiter's four largest moons are Io, Europa, Ganymede, and Callisto. Europa is smaller than our moon, but the other three are larger. These four moons are very different from one another. For instance, Io is covered in volcanoes. Europa's surface is mostly water ice. Callisto is probably the most ancient, and it's covered in craters.

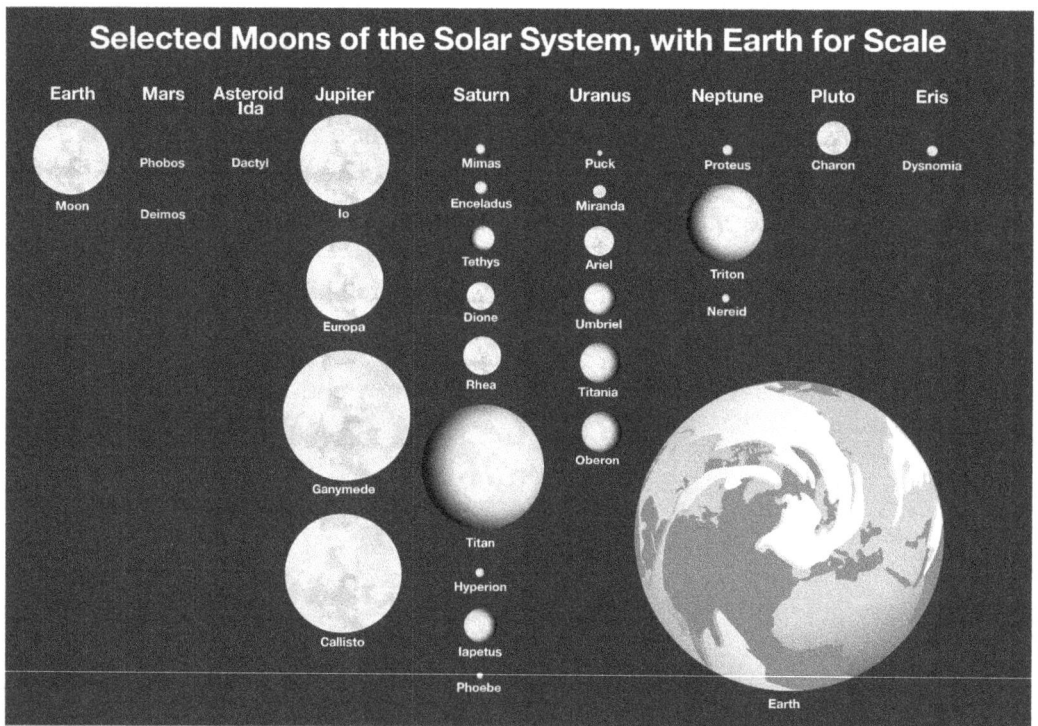

7. Based on the passage and the image, which of Jupiter's four largest moons is NOT bigger than Earth's moon?
    - **A.** Io
    - **B.** Europa
    - **C.** Ganymede
    - **D.** Callisto

8. Based on the image, what other planet has a moon that is much larger than Earth's moon?
    - **A.** Mars
    - **B.** Neptune
    - **C.** Uranus
    - **D.** Saturn

DESCRIBE & MAKE CONNECTIONS IN TEXT

RI.3.8 Describe the logical connection between particular sentences and paragraphs in a text (e.g., comparison, cause/effect, first/second/third in a sequence)

Directions: Read the passage and answer the questions that follow.

Passage 1: One Arm, All Heart

1 Bethany Hamilton was born in Hawaii in 1990. Bethany and her brothers all learned to surf at very young ages. By the young age of eight years old, Bethany Hamilton was a competitive surfer.

2 Bethany was home schooled so that she could pursue her passion of surfing. In 1999, Bethany became sponsored by the Hanalei Surf Company. As a competitor, Bethany was beating people who had been surfing much longer than she had and had much more experience.

3 In October of 2003, Bethany went surfing with her friend Alana, Alana's father, and Alana's brother at Tunnels Beach in Hawaii. Bethany was lying on her surfboard in the ocean when she suddenly felt an intense pressure on her arm while being pulled back and forth. Bethany noticed that the water around her was turning red, but she surprisingly didn't feel any pain. It was her friends who realized that her arm had been sundered to almost her shoulder.

4 Eventually, it was determined that Bethany was attacked by a 14-foot tiger shark. As a result of the attack, massive amounts of blood were extravasated from her arm, and Bethany had several surgeries. But, she was discharged from the hospital a few days later.

5 Despite losing her arm, Bethany pledged to get back to surfing as soon as possible. Just one month later, Bethany returned to the waves. In no time, she was back to competing and winning awards. Bethany Hamilton was back and better than ever.

1. Why does the author include the information in Paragraph 2?
    A. To show that Bethany was a poor student
    B. To describe Bethany's passion for surfing
    C. To show Bethany was bad at surfing
    D. To introduce the problem

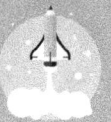

2. What is the relationship between Paragraph 3 and Paragraph 4?

    A. Paragraph 3 introduces a problem, and Paragraph 4 introduces the solution.
    B. Paragraph 3 shows a cause, and Paragraph 4 shows the effect.
    C. Paragraph 3 introduces a problem, and Paragraph 4 introduces a lesson..
    D. Paragraph 3 introduces the characters and setting, but Paragraph 4 introduces the problem and solution.

3. Why is Paragraph 5 included in the passage? Explain your reasoning using details from the passage.

___

4. What are the effects of the shark attack? Choose all that apply.
    ☐ Bethany can no longer surf.
    ☐ Bethany undergoes many surgeries.
    ☐ Bethany loses her arm.
    ☐ Bethany has to stay in the hospital for several months.
    ☐ Bethany loses a lot of blood.
    ☐ Bethany makes a promise to herself to return to surfing

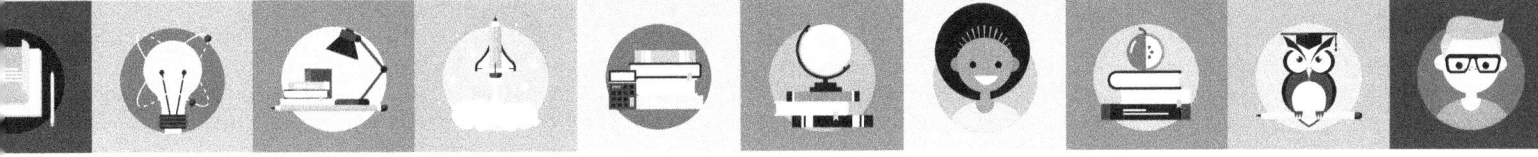

Passage 2: Don't Give Up

1   Patricia Polacco was born on a farm in Michigan in 1944. She lived in Union City, Michigan with her parents and **beloved** grandparents. Patricia grew up in a storytelling family where she heard the most fascinating stories. Her babushka's (grandmother's) stories were some of her favorites.

2   Patricia's parents were divorced when she was just three years old. As a result, Patricia and her brother spent much of their childhood living in two places. They spent the school year in Oakland, California where their mother lived, and they spent the summers in Michigan where their father and grandparents lived.

3   Elementary school was very hard for Patricia. She tried very hard to learn how to read and write, but she just couldn't do it. The harder reading and writing became, the more Patricia concentrated on her drawing. She just loved to draw.

4   Throughout her childhood, Patricia was constantly teased and bullied. Children would call her names like "dumb" and "stupid." She especially hated to read out loud because she always made mistakes, and the teacher had to help her sound out every single word. Eventually, she despised going to school.

5   It wasn't until Patricia was fourteen years old that she learned how to read. One of Patricia's teachers recognized that she had a learning disability called **dyslexia.** Finally, Patricia was able to get the help she needed.

6   Now, Patricia Polacco is a famous writer of children's books. She has written several books such as *Thank You, Mr. Falker* and *The Keeping Quilt.* Many of her books tell about the stories her grandparents told her as a child. Her books also tell about her struggles with learning to read and how she was bullied. Patricia is a wonderful example that if we work hard and never give up, we can **accomplish** great things!

5. Why is it important to mention in Paragraph 3 that school was very hard for Patricia?
    A. The author wanted us to infer that Patricia is a bad student.
    B. The author wanted us to infer that if Patricia tried harder in school, she would have learned how to read.
    C. It gives the reader interesting background information about Patricia.
    D. The author wanted us to understand that even though Patricia tried very hard in school, she still couldn't learn how to read.

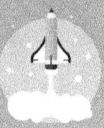

6. How does the information in Paragraph 2 build on the information in Paragraph 1?
   A. Paragraph 1 introduces Patricia and Paragraph 2 tells more about her childhood.
   B. Paragraph 1 introduces the cause and Paragraph 2 presents the effect.
   C. Paragraph 2 presents the solution for the problem introduced in Paragraph 1.
   D. Paragraph 1 introduces why Patricia loves stories and Paragraph 2 explains the effect of this.

7. Even though Patricia has a learning disability, she is now a famous author of children's books. What are 2 factors that helped Patricia to become a famous author?

_____
_____
_____
_____

8. Why does the author include Paragraph 4?
   A. To show that Patricia could have learned how to read if she tried harder
   B. To show why Patricia hated school
   C. To explain why Patricia gave up
   D. To show readers that bullying is bad

COMPARE AND CONTRAST KEY POINTS IN TWO TEXTS

RI.3.9 Compare and contrast the most important points and key details presented in two texts on the same topic.

Directions: Read the passages and answer the questions that follow.

Passage 1: Cell Phones Have No Place at School

1   School is a place to learn, and cell phones can prevent students from learning. For this reason, students should not bring cell phones to school.

2   Cell phones cause too much temptation. Students want to see if their friends are texting them, play fun games, watch videos, or check their social media apps. If students decide to look at their phones, they aren't able to pay attention to their assignments or to what the teacher is saying. They may miss important information.

3   Even if students do avoid the temptation to look at their cell phones, they may be distracted by thinking about checking their cell phones or wondering if someone is texting them.

4   Sometimes, students' cell phones go off in the middle of class, which can also be disruptive and distracting. Anything that can interrupt learning has no place in the classroom.

5   Lastly, some students use cell phones to share answers on assignments and tests. They may text each other answers or send one another pictures of assignments. Some students might also use their cell phones to look up answers for assignments and tests. When students cheat, they don't learn the information for themselves. This is another reason that cell phones can prevent kids from doing what they're supposed to be doing at school: learning.

Passage 2: Should Cell Phones Be Allowed at School?

1   Many people disagree on the issue of whether or not cell phones should be allowed at school. There are convincing arguments on both sides.

2   It's true that cell phones can be very distracting for students. If students are too busy texting, playing games, or checking social media, they aren't as focused on their schoolwork as they should be. They could miss valuable information or not learn something that they will need later on. This can have a negative impact on their grades and on their education.

3   On the other hand, students may need to contact their parents after or even during school. What if an emergency happens? What if the student's after-school activity gets

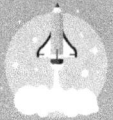

cancelled and they need a parent to pick them up earlier? What if the parent needs to tell the student that someone else will be picking them up after school? Parents need to be able to get in contact with their children.

4   Students should be able to have their cell phones at school as a safety measure or in case they need to speak to their parents. But they shouldn't be allowed to have their cell phones out during class at all. Students must be responsible enough to have their cell phones at school without letting them distract from the purpose of attending school, which is learning.

1. What is a key detail that is mentioned in both passages?
   A. Students may use cell phones to cheat on assignments or tests.
   B. Students need to be able to contact their parents in case of emergency.
   C. Cell phones can distract students from learning.
   D. Cell phones sometimes go off in class, causing a disruption.

2. On which of the following statements would the author of Passage 1 and the author of Passage 2 disagree?
   A. Students may be distracted by texting and social media.
   B. Students shouldn't have their phones out in class at all.
   C. Cell phones should not be allowed to disrupt learning.
   D. Students should not be allowed to bring phones to school.

3. What is the main difference between Passage 1 and Passage 2? Explain.

_____
_____
_____
_____
_____
_____

4. Which of the following arguments is mentioned in Passage 1, but is not mentioned in Passage 2?
   A. Students may text each other answers or send one another pictures of assignments.
   B. Students could miss important information.
   C. Cell phones are distracting in school.
   D. The purpose of going to school is to learn.

5. List two arguments that are mentioned in Passage 2 but are not mentioned in Passage 1.
   ☐ Students may need to contact parents in case of an emergency.
   ☐ Students may be distracted by thinking about checking their cell phones or wondering if someone is texting them.
   ☐ When students cheat, they don't learn the information for themselves.
   ☐ Students should be able to have their cell phones at school as a safety measure or in case they need to speak to their parents.

6. The author of Passage 1 mentions that students may use their phones to cheat on assignments or tests. How would the author of Passage 2 most likely respond to this point?
   A. That's why students shouldn't be allowed to have phones at school.
   B. That's not as important as students being able to contact their parents.
   C. This may be true, but students should not be allowed to have their cell phones out in class.
   D. It's unlikely that cell phones would be used in this way.

7. Which passage do you agree with the most? Which arguments convinced you to agree with this passage?

   _____
   _____
   _____
   _____
   _____
   _____

8. Both authors agree that the purpose of school is _____.
   A. Preparing students for adulthood.
   B. Learning.
   C. To understand when you should and should not use your phone during class.
   D. Socializing.

LANGUAGE

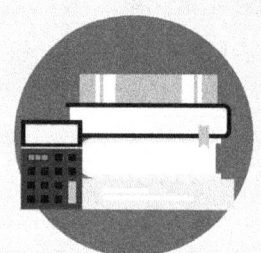  

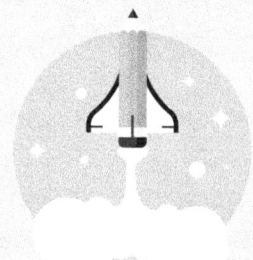  

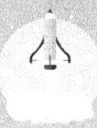

DEMONSTRATE COMMAND OF GRAMMAR & USAGE

L.1.1: Demonstrate command of the conventions of standard English grammar and usage when writing or speaking.

1. What is the function of an adjective?
   - **A.** To describe a noun
   - **B.** To tell about an action
   - **C.** To name a person, place, or thing
   - **D.** To take the place of a noun

2. What is the adjective in the sentence below?
   The large dog ran across the street.
   - **A.** street
   - **B.** across
   - **C.** large
   - **D.** dog

3. What is the pronoun in the sentence below?
   Mr. White was scared of dogs, so he ran away.
   - **A.** Mr. White
   - **B.** he
   - **C.** dogs
   - **D.** ran

4. Choose the best adjective to fill in the blank.
   The horse was _____ than the dog.
   - **A.** big
   - **B.** bigger
   - **C.** biggest
   - **D.** more big

5. How would you change the noun bus to make it plural?
   - **A.** Add another -s
   - **B.** Double the -s, then add -es
   - **C.** Add an apostrophe and another -s
   - **D.** Add -es at the end

6. Complete the sentence below with the correct verb.
   I _____ to school yesterday.
   - **A.** walk
   - **B.** walked
   - **C.** walking
   - **D.** will walk

7. Complete the sentence below with the correct verb.
   We will _____ our favorite songs tomorrow in music class.
   - **A.** sing
   - **B.** sang
   - **C.** sung
   - **D.** singing

LANGUAGE

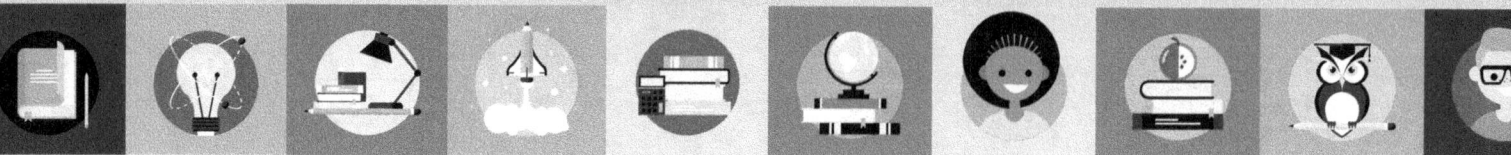

8. Choose the correct pronoun to agree with the antecedent in the sentence below.
   Michael and Jose both ride _____ bikes to school.
   - **A.** his
   - **B.** our
   - **C.** their
   - **D.** him

9. Complete the sentence below with a coordinating conjunction.
   For my birthday, I want to go to Disney World, _____ I want my best friends to come with me.
   - **A.** but
   - **B.** and
   - **C.** yet
   - **D.** nor

10. Complete the sentence below with a subordinating conjunction.
    _____ school, John always goes to soccer practice.
    - **A.** Although
    - **B.** Whenever
    - **C.** While
    - **D.** After

11. What type of sentence is the sentence below?
    Joey likes to read books, and he also likes to watch movies.
    - **A.** Simple
    - **B.** Compound
    - **C.** Complex
    - **D.** None of the above

12. What type of sentence is the sentence below?
    Jenna also likes to read books, such as chapter books.
    - **A.** Simple
    - **B.** Compound
    - **C.** Complex
    - **D.** None of the above

KNOW CAPITALIZATION, PUNCTUATION & SPELLING

L.1.2 Demonstrate command of the conventions of standard English capitalization, punctuation, and spelling when writing.

1. Which of the following titles is correctly capitalized?
    - **A.** *The Lion, The Witch, And The Wardrobe*
    - **B.** *The Lion, the Witch, And the Wardrobe*
    - **C.** *The Lion, the Witch, and the Wardrobe*
    - **D.** *the Lion, the Witch, and the Wardrobe*

2. Choose the address that uses commas correctly.
    - **A.** 1520 King Street, Orlando, FL, 32825
    - **B.** 1520 King Street Orlando, FL 32825
    - **C.** 1520, King Street, Orlando, FL 32825
    - **D.** 1520 King Street, Orlando, FL 32825

3. Which of the following sentences uses quotation marks and commas correctly?
    - **A.** "I want to go home," said the little girl.
    - **B.** "I want to go home", said the little girl.
    - **C.** "I want to go home, said" the little girl.
    - **D.** "I want to go home, said the little girl."

4. Which of the following sentences uses quotation marks and commas correctly?
    - **A.** "After you finish your vegetables" Mom said, "you can have dessert."
    - **B.** "After you finish your vegetables", Mom said "you can have dessert."
    - **C.** "After you finish your vegetables," Mom said, "you can have dessert."
    - **D.** "After you finish your vegetables Mom said," you can have dessert.

5. Complete the following sentence. The _____ car was shiny and red.
    - **A.** mans
    - **B.** man's
    - **C.** mans'
    - **D.** mans's

6. Complete the following sentence. Students were not allowed in the _____ lounge.
    - **A.** teachers
    - **B.** teacher's
    - **C.** teachers'
    - **D.** teachers's

LANGUAGE

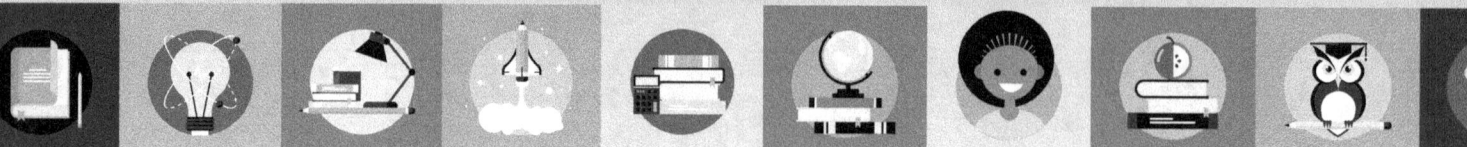

7. Which of the following sentences is correct?
    A. It always wakes me up when my sister cries.
    B. It always wakes me up when my sister cry's.
    C. It always wakes me up when my sister crys.
    D. It always wakes me up when my sister crie's.

8. What suffix should be added to push to make it past tense?
    Yesterday, I _____ my sister on the swing.
    A. -ness
    B. -ly
    C. -ing
    D. -ed

9. What suffix should be added to sit to make it present tense?
    The class is _____ in the gym until the rain stops.
    A. -ness
    B. -ly
    C. -ing
    D. -ed

10. What suffix should be added to happy to refer to the state of being happy?
    The family was filled with love and _____ when the new baby was born.
    A. -ness
    B. -ly
    C. -ing
    D. -ed

USE APPROPRIATE LANGUAGE CONVENTIONS

L.2.3: Use knowledge of language and its conventions when writing, speaking, reading, or listening.

1. It was finally the big day! Alexis was turning twelve.

   She expected her parents and friends to be as excited about her birthday as she was, but no one mentioned her birthday at breakfast. When Alexis got to school, she was sure her friends would run up to her and say, "Happy birthday". However, no one did.

   After school, Alexis went to soccer practice. She was sad and confused that her birthday had been forgotten. The soccer coach drove Alexis home from practice. Alexis was ready to go to sleep and forget the worst birthday ever. As soon as the coach opened the door, Alexis heard, "HAPPY BIRTHDAY!" and saw balloons, cake, presents, and all of her family and friends. She was definitely _____.

   Choose the word that **best** fills in the blank to describe how Alexis feels at the end of the passage?
   - **A.** sad
   - **B.** confused
   - **C.** upset
   - **D.** surprised

2. Starfish are truly _____ animals. Some of them have five arms, but others have as many as 40. If a starfish ever loses an arm, it can grow it back. Unlike most animals, starfish don't have blood or bones.

   Choose the word that **best** fits in the blank to complete the sentence.
   - **A.** beautiful
   - **B.** unique
   - **C.** boring
   - **D.** common

LANGUAGE

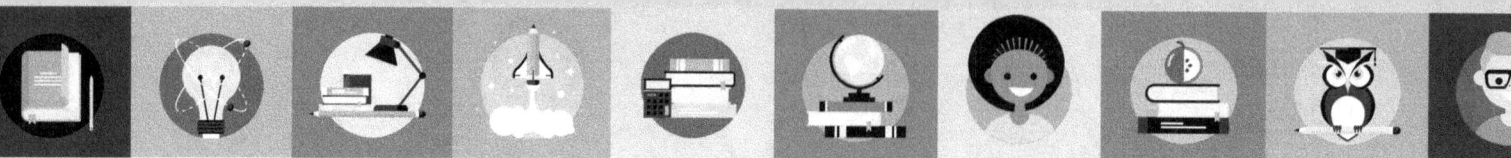

3. In a village long ago, there lived a massive dragon. He was taller than the tallest castle in the kingdom, and he could breathe fire for miles. Many brave knights had tried to defeat the dragon, but no one could do it. There was a rumor that the dragon was going to destroy the entire village with his fiery breath. All of the villagers were so _____ that they had nightmares for weeks.

   Choose the word that best fits in the blank to describe how the villagers feel about the dragon.
   - **A.** excited
   - **B.** terrified
   - **C.** nervous
   - **D.** gloomy

4. Many people believe that Michael Jordan is the greatest basketball player ever. But when he was fifteen-years-old, he tried out for his high school basketball team and didn't make it. After finding out he didn't make the team, Jordan went home, went into his bedroom, and cried.

   Jordan could have given up. He could have decided he would never be a great basketball player. Instead, he used not making the team as _____. It made him work even harder. Whenever he didn't feel like practicing his shot or lifting weights, Jordan closed his eyes. He remembered how he felt when his name wasn't on the team list. That was enough _____ to keep going. The next year, Jordan made the high school basketball team and quickly became their best player.

   Choose the word that best fits the blanks to complete the sentences.
   - **A.** motivation
   - **B.** disappointment
   - **C.** happiness
   - **D.** defeat

5. A big scoop of ice cream fell off Melissa's ice cream cone. She felt _____ as she watched her ice cream land on the grass.

   Which word best completes the sentence and describes the girl's feelings?
   - **A.** tired
   - **B.** confused
   - **C.** sad
   - **D.** worried

6. What sentence does NOT describe the ocean?
    A. The ocean contains waves, big and small.
    B. I love playing in the ocean.
    C. The ocean is a huge body of salt water.
    D. The ocean is a large area of sea

7. Which sentence best describes a happy puppy?
    A. We could hear him whining from the other room.
    B. He was running faster than the speed of light.
    C. He growled like a lion and showed his teeth.
    D. He jumped around like a bunny rabbit, wagging his tail back and forth.

8. What does this phrase "You crack me up," mean?
    A. You make them laugh.
    B. You broke something.
    C. You hurt them.
    D. You made them cry.

9. What does the phrase "to go the extra mile" mean?"
    A. Walk a long distance.
    B. Keep running after everyone else stops.
    C. Do more than what is expected or required.
    D. Try your best.

10. What does the following sentence mean?

    Miguel stayed home from school because he was feeling a little under the weather.

    A. Miguel stayed home from school because it was too cold.
    B. Miguel stayed home from school because he didn't feel like going anywhere.
    C. Miguel stayed home from school because it might rain.
    D. Miguel stayed home from school because he felt sick.

LANGUAGE

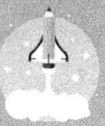

DETERMINE MEANING OF UNKNOWN WORD/S IN CONTEXT

L.3.4: Determine or clarify the meaning of unknown and multiple-meaning words and phrases based on grade 3 reading and content, choosing flexibly from a range of strategies.

1. Fish, whales, and dolphins are aquatic animals.
   Based on the context clues, what do you think the word **aquatic** means?
   - **A.** Large
   - **B.** Small
   - **C.** Water
   - **D.** Gentle

2. Mom had to **sterilize** the baby's bottle to make sure it was clean.
   What does the word **sterilize** mean in this sentence?
   - **A.** Clean
   - **B.** Buy
   - **C.** Find
   - **D.** Look at

3. Elephants and hippos have a **pewter** color to their skin.
   What does the word **pewter** mean in this sentence? How do the context clues help you?

   _____
   _____
   _____

4. Our waitress was in a bad mood and was not very **cordial** to us.
   What does the word **cordial** mean in this sentence?
   - **A.** Rude
   - **B.** Talkative
   - **C.** Polite
   - **D.** Bored

5. Jimmy was terrible at crossword puzzles, but his sister Julie was very **adept** at them.
   What do you think the word **adept** means in this sentence?
   - **A.** Terrible
   - **B.** Good
   - **C.** Okay
   - **D.** Interested

6. The base word **agree** means to have the same opinion about something. What do you think the word **agreeable** means?
    A. Happy
    B. Argumentative
    C. Not able to share the same opinion
    D. Able to share the same opinion

7. The base word **complete** means finished. What does the word **incomplete** mean?

8. What is the difference in meaning between the words **preheat** and **reheat**?

9. What root word do the following words have in common: **Section, bisect, dissect**

    What does the word **bisect** mean?

10. What suffix should be added to happy to refer to the state of being happy? The family was filled with love and _____ when the new baby was born.
    A. -ness
    B. -ly
    C. -ing
    D. -ed

LANGUAGE

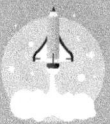

UNDERSTAND WORD RELATIONSHIPS AND NUANCES IN MEANING

L.3.5: Demonstrate understanding of word relationships and nuances in word meanings.

1. What does the bold phrase mean in the following sentence?
   After Chloe and her best friend Naya had a big argument, Chloe wanted to **take steps** to fix their friendship.
   - **A.** Go for a walk
   - **B.** Take action
   - **C.** Run away
   - **D.** Walk to Naya's house

2. What does the bold phrase mean in the following sentence?
   Max was bigger and stronger than his brother Peter, so Max had the **upper hand** in competitions like wrestling.
   - **A.** The advantage
   - **B.** His hand was on top
   - **C.** His hand was bigger
   - **D.** The disadvantage

3. Is the following sentence figurative or literal? Explain why.
   After practice, Sarah was so hungry she could eat a horse.

   _____
   _____
   _____

4. Is the following sentence figurative or literal? Explain why.
   The boy was as tall as a giraffe.

   _____
   _____
   _____

5. Which word has a similar meaning to **annoyed**?
   - **A.** Amused
   - **B.** Aggravated
   - **C.** Joyful
   - **D.** Confused

LANGUAGE

6. Which word is similar in meaning to **massive**?
    A. Short
    B. Long
    C. Huge
    D. Tiny

7. Which word means the opposite of **fascinated**?
    A. Scared
    B. Entertained
    C. Happy
    D. Bored

8. Which word could replace the bold word to describe the situation in more detail.
   The boy happily **walked** home.
    A. ran
    B. skipped
    C. stomped
    D. tiptoed

9. Which sentence seems to suggest that Anthony is *most* upset? Explain why.
    A. Anthony was mad.
    B. Anthony was furious.
    C. Anthony was displeased.
    D. Anthony was irritated.

_____

_____

_____

10. Which sentence has a more positive implication?
    A. The girl frowned.
    B. The girl smirked.
    C. The girl laughed.
    D. The girl stared.

11. Find the synonym for the bold word in the sentence below.
    The **sluggish** turtle finished the race last.
    A. Slow
    B. Fast
    C. Speedy
    D. Friendly

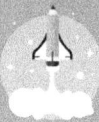

KNOW ACADEMIC/DOMAIN-SPECIFIC WORDS

L.3.6: Acquire and use accurately conversational, general academic, and domain specific words and phrases as found in grade appropriate texts, including those that signal spatial and temporal relationships (e.g., After dinner that night we went looking for them).

1. In which of the following classes would you most likely use the word "simile?"
   - **A.** Math
   - **B.** English/Language Arts
   - **C.** Music
   - **D.** Science

2. Which of the following words means "the total amount when adding two or more numbers?"
   - **A.** Perimeter
   - **B.** Area
   - **C.** Sum
   - **D.** Estimate

3. In which class would you most likely learn about "amphibians?"
   - **A.** Math
   - **B.** English/Language Arts
   - **C.** Music
   - **D.** Science

4. What does it mean if your teacher asks you to "use context clues" to figure out the meaning of a word?
   - **A.** Look up the word in the dictionary.
   - **B.** Ask your friend what the word means.
   - **C.** Figure out what the word means based on the information in the sentence.
   - **D.** Raise your hand and ask the teacher for the meaning of the word.

5. In which class would you most likely learn about "antecedents?"
   - **A.** Math
   - **B.** English/Language Arts
   - **C.** Music
   - **D.** Science

6. What does the word "contrast" mean?
    - **A.** Describe similarities between two or more things.
    - **B.** Describe differences between two or more things.
    - **C.** A word that has the same meaning as another word.
    - **D.** List events in order.

7. Choose the most accurate definition of solar system.
    - **A.** The planets and moons that orbit the sun.
    - **B.** The organs and glands in the body that are responsible for digestion.
    - **C.** The process of water circulating between the oceans, atmosphere, and land.
    - **D.** The different types of clouds, including cumulus and cirrus.

8. Select the word or phrase that best completes the sentence below.
    The student who was _____ me in line kept stepping on the back of my shoes.
    - **A.** in front of
    - **B.** behind
    - **C.** next to
    - **D.** to the right of

9. Select the word or phrase that best completes the sentence below.
    We had to wake up early enough to get breakfast _____ school.
    - **A.** in the meantime
    - **B.** during
    - **C.** after
    - **D.** before

10. Select the word or phrase that best completes the sentence below.
    The plane flew far _____ my head.
    - **A.** outside
    - **B.** above
    - **C.** parallel to
    - **D.** in front of

LANGUAGE

ANSWER EXPLANATIONS

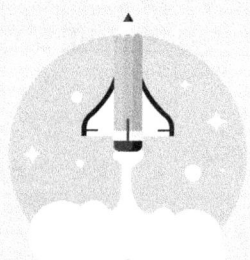

READING LITERATURE
RL.1.1 Ask & Answer Questions Using Text Evidence

1. Part A- **C.** The man believes the cheeses will meet him at the marketplace, which is what he tells them to do when he lets them go.

Part B- **A.** Once the man believes that the cheeses can find their way to the market alone, he states: "Well, then, if you can go to market alone, so can the other cheeses, and I will send them along after you." This statement proves that the man is confident the cheeses will find their way and meet him there.

2. **B.** When the author tell us that the cheeses roll into different bushes, but the man doesn't notice this, we begin to realize that the cheeses will never make their way all the way down to market.

3. After the first cheese escapes, the man says, "So you can run to the market alone, can you? I wish I had known that before. It would have saved me the trouble of carrying you. Well then, if you can go to market alone, so can the other cheeses, and I will send them along after you" (Paragraph 3). As long as students identify any segment of this quote and are able to explain their thinking, the answer should be considered correct. This quote shows that the man is tired of carrying the cheeses and that he believes the first cheese escaped to go to the market. For these reasons, he lets the other cheeses go as well.

4. **B.** Since it is already evening and the cheeses haven't arrived, and since the title of the passage is "The Cheeses That Ran Away," it can be inferred that the man will never find his cheeses. Also, we know that when he rolled the cheeses down the hill, the man didn't realize that some of the cheeses rolled into bushes instead.

5. The man's opinion is that the kettle will follow him home. He gives the kettle directions to where he lives (para 5), and he tells his wife that the kettle is on its way, and "be along in good time." (para 6).

The wife disagrees with the husband and doesn't believe the kettle will arrive at the home. She asks the husband where he left it and "hurries off to get it." The passage also states, "She was not so sure about its coming as he was."

6. In Paragraph 2, the man realizes that the kettle has three legs, while he only has two. This leads him to the decision that the kettle should carry him instead of the other way around.

7. **B.** Both the cheeses and the kettle disobey their owners. The cheeses are told to go to the market and run away instead. The kettle is told to go to the man's home and refuses to walk.

8. Part A- **C.** The woman doesn't think the kettle will come home, which is why she repeatedly asks the man where he has left the kettle.

Part B- **B.** The woman goes to get the kettle and bring it home. After asking her husband where the kettle is located, she "hurries off to get it."

RL.1. 2. Recount Stories & Determine Theme

1. (2) The Grasshopper says there's no need to worry about winter because they have plenty of food at present.

(5) The Grasshopper has no food in the winter and begins to die of starvation, while the ants continue to eat the grain and corn they collected in the summer.

2. Answers may vary. A main lesson is that you should always work hard and prepare for difficult times during the good times. (This is conveyed as the Grasshopper refuses to prepare for the winter and faces the consequences, while the Ant diligently prepares and has plenty of food during the winter.)

3. **D.** We see that the Grasshopper should have prepared like the Ant because the Grasshopper has no food and is starving.

4. The Grasshopper says that there is plenty of food right now, and later he says that winter is still many days away.

5. Answers may vary. One lesson is to listen to your parents. (Icarus is told by his father not to fly too close to the sun, but he ignores the warning and falls into the ocean.)

6. **C.** Icarus doesn't listen to his father. The wax begins to melt, the seagull feathers begin to fall off, and Icarus falls into the ocean and drowns. This teaches the lesson that Icarus should have listened to Daedalus, and children should listen to their parents.

7. **B.** The beginning of the passage states that Daedalus and Icarus are imprisoned because Daedalus is a very talented inventor, and King Minos wants Daedalus to only make inventions for him.

8. **D.** Only the title "The Disobedient Son" does a good job of summarizing the story and conveying its overall message. "Flying," "The Inventor and his Inventions," and "The Greedy King Minos" are too specific and not representative of the story as a whole.

RL.1.3 Describe Characters & Explain Their Actions

1. **B.** They both have positive attitudes. Each time a problem happens during the camp out, Jessica and Tia do their best to stay positive and still enjoy themselves.

2. **A.** She's a good friend. The passage also says that Tia didn't want Jessica to feel bad about forgetting the marshmallows, which shows she cares about her friend's feelings.

3. Answers may vary. Students should say that they would or would not like to be friends with Tia and Jessica, and they should provide at least one detail from the passage to support their response. For example, students might say that they would like to be friends with the girls because they seem nice (like when Tia didn't want Jessica to feel bad) and try to make the best of any situation (like when they try to enjoy the smores even though they aren't the same).

4. **2nd and 4th Choice.** Both of these details show the girls being flexible by adapting to the problems that occur on the camp out.

5. At the beginning, Lauren doesn't like raking leaves. (She pouts and sighs while dragging the rake "for what felt like the hundredth time.") After spending the day raking leaves with Drew, Lauren learns to enjoy raking. (She smiles when her dad says raking leaves should be her chore from now on and says, "Raking leaves isn't so bad."). There are other details that could be added, but these are some of the main ones.

6. Part A- **A.** Like Tia and Jessica in the first passage, Drew can make the best of a bad situation. He makes raking leaves fun by playing games and having a positive attitude about raking.

Part B- **C.** Drew responds enthusiastically when Lauren asks if he's sure about helping with the leaves, and he immediately suggests a way to make raking more fun.

7. Drew is a good friend because he volunteers to help Lauren with raking the leaves, and he tries to cheer her up and make her task more fun with games like leaf jumping and races.

8. Lauren: She doesn't like raking leaves.

Supporting Detail: She sighs and pouts while raking the leaves, and she can't believe that anyone would volunteer to help with something so boring.

Drew: He doesn't mind raking leaves.

Supporting Detail: He volunteers to help Lauren. When she asks if he's sure, he enthusiastically says, "Of course!" Immediately, he begins finding ways to make raking the leaves more fun.

RL.2.4 Determine Word Meaning In Context

1. **A.** The author is nervous. The text says that the author is worried, and it also says that the author has practiced for weeks. We know that she's prepared, but she's still nervous that something might go wrong.

2. Fell asleep. Readers can guess that "dozed off" means fell asleep because the text says that Josie was bored and tired.

3. The phrases "straight down" and "into the water" tell readers that plunge means to fall down. The fact that the bridge is old and Peter must walk carefully are additional hints.

4. The author compares his struggles in math class to climbing a mountain. He says, "We all have challenges in life. We all have our mountains to climb. For me, it's math class." He also talks about working hard and eventually "reaching the top."

5. **A.** Fast. Liz wins every race, and it's never even close. This tells us that Liz is very fast.

6. **C.** Courage. Peter is the only one who is brave enough to go into Old Man Frank's yard; everyone else is too scared.

7. **B.** "...and listened for the sound of Old Man Frank yelling." The fact that they are listening for a noise shows readers that "caught our breath" means to be silent and wait.

8. Answers may vary. There are several clues: the phrase, "Except he wasn't yelling" shows that the boys were wrong in their assumptions (guesses) about Old Man Frank. The sentence, "It seemed like he wasn't so scary after all," also indicates that the boys had guessed incorrectly. Details like Old Man Frank asking friendly questions and telling stories about his childhood provide additional clues.

RL.2.5 Identify & Understand Parts Of Texts

1. **B.** A poem. Poems are divided into stanzas like stories are divided into paragraphs.

2. **B.** Scene. Plays are divided into scenes like stories are divided into paragraphs.

3. **C.** Line breaks are used to enhance ideas and meaning in a poem.

4. At the beginning of the story, so readers

understand where the story takes place and who the characters are. It would be confusing if setting and characters were introduced later in the story.

5. At the end, because the story is over once the problem is solved. There's no reason to continue the story when there's no problem to solve.

6. **B.** There are four stanzas in this poem

7. **C.** The little master should appreciate that the sheep grows wool that will be used to make the master's clothing.

8. **B.** These lines show that when spring is over, the sheep's wool is cut to warm the master through the cold winter. While the sheep may seem lazy in the spring, he benefits the master in the winter.

RL.2.6 Identify Point Of View of Self & Author/Characters

1. **C.** Point of view is who is narrating or telling the story. It's the perspective from which the story is told.

2. **B.** Third-person point of view is when a character is not an active participant in the story. Words like "he," "she," and "they" are used.

3. Part A- **C.** A puppy is the narrator of the story.

Part B- **B.** The man who brings the puppy home. It isn't clear that the narrator is a puppy until the man says, "Hi, little puppy!"

4. **A.** The story is told from the first-person point of view. The narrator, the puppy, is an active participant in the story, and he uses words like "I."

5. The author makes the reader feel sad and worried for the puppy. Details like the puppy being cold, people honking and yelling at the puppy, and the puppy being hungry create this feeling.

6. **C.** The puppy is cold because of the rain, and he's trying to find shelter.

7. Part A- **B** "...but she didn't look very happy." This quote shows that the woman will allow the puppy to stay at her house, but she doesn't truly want him to be there.

Part B- **A.** The woman doesn't know that the dog is homeless. This might make her feel more sorry for the puppy and want to help him.

8. All of the other human characters in the story don't like the dog and don't want to help him. People honk at the puppy, and someone yells, "Get out of the way!" Another man tells the puppy, "Get lost!" Susie, the man's wife, says, "Are you crazy?" when the man brings the puppy home. Only the man is nice to the puppy, calling him cute, asking if he has anywhere to go, and bringing him home.

RL.3.7 Identify How Illustrations Convey Information

1. Answers may vary. Nathan and Julie got off the school bus, and they're excited about having a great first day of school.

2. Answers may vary. Nathan and Julie seem like they feel happy in this picture. The twins are smiling. They are walking with big strides, or possibly skipping. The text says that they're finally in the same class, their new teacher seems nice, and most of their best friends are in the class too. It also says that they're confident third grade will be a good year.

3. Some of the clues that the author gives that prove Nathan and Julie feel like they will have a great year in third grade is: they've never been in the same class before, but they are this year; their new teacher seems very nice, and many of their best friends are also in their class. In the pictures, both Nathan and Julie are smiling, they're holding hands, and they're walking with big strides or skipping. This shows they are confident about having a great third grade year.

4. **B.** In comparison to the person in the photo, this image emphasizes the dog's massive size (which is described in the text).

5. **D.** As the text also explains, this image shows that the dog is sweet and loving. His hands are on the girl's shoulders, almost like a hug. It looks like he's being very gentle despite his size.

6. The purpose of this image is to help readers visualize the information in the text (or to further emphasize the information in the text). In the text, the writer explains that although her dog is huge, he's very sweet and loving. The image shows that the dog is enormous as well, but it also shows that the dog is loving and gentle. He's not mean or scary, as some people assume based on his size.

7. Answers may vary. The boy looks as though he's feeling scared or nervous. Evidence that the boy looks scared or nervous is that his eyes are wide, his mouth is curved and his teeth are showing, his hands are up to defend himself, the bee is looking at him angrily, and it looks as though several more bees are coming out of the beehive.

RL. 3.9 Compare & Contrast Narratives

1. Both the farmer and the dog are greedy and want more than they already have. The farmer wants more than one golden egg each day, and the dog wants a bigger bone. They both attempt to gain more and instead lose what they already had (the goose for the farmer and the bone for the dog).

2. Part A- **B.** The golden goose and the farmer live on a farm.

Part B- **A.** The dog is walking past a river when he thinks his reflection is another dog with a bigger bone.

3. Part A- **D.** Both characters should have been grateful for what they have instead of being greedy. Then the farmer would still have his golden goose and the dog would still have his bone. Instead, both characters end up with nothing.

Part B- **D.** The fact that the farmer's goose dies at the end of the story develops the theme that the farmer should have been grateful for what he had instead of being greedy.

4. The farmer's decision: To cut open the goose for more eggs

The result: There are no eggs inside the goose, and the goose dies.

The dog's decision: To jump into the river in an attempt to get a bigger bone from the "other dog" (which was really his reflection).

The result: The dog has to frantically swim to shore, loses his bone, and of course does not get a bigger bone either.

5. **A.** In both stories, the conflict occurs as the result of the main characters not being satisfied with what they have.

6. The farmer cut open his goose in hopes of getting more golden eggs. The story explains that the goose only laid one golden egg each day, and the farmer was getting impatient. He wanted more eggs and more money, so he decided to cut open the goose.

7. The dog jumped into the river because he thought his reflection was another dog with a bigger bone than the one he had been given by the butcher. The passage explains that if the dog had thought for a moment, he might have realized his mistake. Instead, he impulsively jumped into the river to try to get the bigger bone from the dog.

8. All options show the farmer and dog are different except the 4th and the 6th option, which contain information that is either incorrect or not in the passage.

READING INFORMATION

RI.1.1 Ask & Answer Questions Using Text Evidence

1. **B.** The starfish is not a fish. The passage explains that scientists are trying to change the name to "sea star" since starfish are not actually fish.

2. **C.** The passage mentions that starfish use their colors as camouflage and to scare off predators and that starfish have hard, bony skin that can protect them from predators. However, starfish don't have sharp spikes on their arms.

3. Answers may vary. Some possible answers are:
1) The starfish doesn't have blood or brains.

2) The starfish can regrow its arms and even grow a whole new starfish from its arm.

3) Starfish have one eye on the tip of each arm and can't see color.

4. The text says that many starfish have 5 arms, but some species of starfish have 10, 20, or even 40 arms.

5. **(2)** The virus makes the starfish weak.

(4) The starfish develops white sores on its body.

(5) The arms sometimes rip off and walk away.

6. **A.** The beginning of the passage states that starfish were dying out "across North America."

7. Part A- **B.** The virus normally affects just one or two species, but now over 20 species have been affected.

Part B- **C.** Scientists think the virus may be spreading more quickly because there are so many starfish packed into small areas.

8. The passage says scientists will continue to study the parvovirus. They want to stop the virus, but if they can't do that, they want to learn more about the virus so they can prevent an outbreak like this one in the future.

RI.1.2 Determine Main Idea & Explain Key Details

1. **B.** The main idea of this passage is that potato chips were an accidental invention. The passage goes on to provide details of exactly how potato chips were accidentally invented.

2. Answers may vary. Possibilities include, "George Crum's customers complained that his fried potatoes were too thick and bland, so he tried to make disgusting fried potatoes that were too thin and too salty," or, "Instead, the customers loved

the fried potatoes, and soon everyone was talking about the tasty new invention of potato chips." Students may also cite the first or last lines of the text, which specifically mention that potato chips were an accidental invention.

3. **C.** This sentence supports the idea that potato chips were not intentionally invented. Instead, they originated from a hotel chef trying to prank some customers who didn't like his food.

4. **D.** The title "Potato Chips: A Happy Accident" represents the main idea of this passage well. The other three choices focus on specific details or aspects of the text that don't represent the text as a whole.

5. **A.** This passage focuses on the idea that although people long believed that Abner Doubleday invented baseball, we don't know who truly invented the sport.

6. Answers may vary. Possibilities include, "Until 2011, popular legend was that a man named Abner Doubleday invented baseball," and, "The rumor was so popular that the Baseball Hall of Fame was opened in Cooperstown, New York, where baseball was supposedly invented." These statements support the idea that the legend of Abner Doubleday was very popular. The following details support the idea that Doubleday didn't invent baseball, and we don't know who did: Historian John Thorn published a book explaining that baseball was played long before 1939, various versions of the game existed in New York, Philadelphia, Massachusetts, and Britain, and John Thorn says the question of who invented baseball is one we may never be able to answer.

7. **D.** The information about Abner Doubleday being a Civil War general does not support or relate to the main idea of the passage (the invention of baseball).

8. **C.** The passage explains that we'll probably never know who invented baseball (mostly because some many variations of it were played in many different locations).

RI.1.3 Describe & Understand Relationships Between Ideas

1. **B.** People believed that the *Titanic* was unsinkable and that nothing bad could happen to the ship, so they didn't have as many lifeboats as they should have.

2. **A.** The passage explains that many historians think the captain of the ship was trying to beat the time of another ship, the *Olympic*.

3. Students should include any two possible details: People believed that the *Titanic* was "the safest ship ever" and it was unsinkable, warnings about icebergs were ignored, the captain was traveling too fast in an effort to beat the time of another ship, and there were only enough lifeboats for half the passengers and crew.

4. Because people believed the *Titanic* was so safe, they made poor decisions. They believed that nothing bad could happen to the ship, so there weren't enough lifeboats on board for everyone. If they hadn't believed that the ship was unsinkable, they might have taken the warnings about icebergs more seriously. The captain might have also traveled more slowly and safely. As a result, damages to the ship and the loss of passengers and crew was much worse than it might have been if people had been more cautious.

5. The entire city was constructed of wood, firefighters were exhausted because of the 20 fires that had occurred the previous week, and firefighters were sent to the wrong neighborhood at first.

6. **C.** The firefighters were sent to the wrong neighborhood at first, so the fire was out of control by the time they finally arrived at the O'Leary home.

7. **B.** The people of Chicago blamed Mrs. O'Leary and her cow. The passage explains that even though Mrs. O'Leary told reporters she was sleeping when the fire started, the newspapers reported that she was milking the cow and the cow kicked over a lantern, starting the destructive fire.

8. When the city was reconstructed, architects built some of the first skyscrapers. The population and economy grew, and the city of Chicago became a great city.

9. Mrs. O'Leary barely left her house after the Chicago Fire. She avoided other people because almost the entire city blamed her for the fire and felt angry about the destruction she had supposedly caused.

10. **B.** The fire finally stopped two days later when it rained.

11. Both passages are about accidents or disasters that are thought to have happened because of a person's actions. The *Titanic* passage reveals that historians believe that the captain of the *Titanic* made the ship go too fast for icy waters, which resulted in the crash. In the Great Chicago Fire passage, the newspapers reported that Ms O'Leary knocked over a lamp which started the fire. Also, in both passages, some people lost their lives because

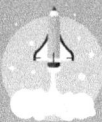

the thing/person(s) expected to save them did not. In the case of the *Titanic,* there were not enough lifeboats on the ship to get all the people to safety. In the Great Chicago Fire, the firefighters were not able to put the fire out (the rain eventually put the fire out), and hundreds of people died.

RI.2.4 Determine Domain-Specific Word Meaning in Context

1. **A.** We know that prevalent means "common" because the next sentence mentions that people visit from all over to see the "many" cacti in these states.

2. **A** succulent is a plant that can store water. The passage explains that cacti can store water in their stems, roots, and leaves and can survive without rain for up to a year.

3. **B.** Hue means color. This part of the passage is about how most cacti are green, but some are slightly different colors like brownish and bluish.

4. **D.** Imagine. The sentence suggests that "picture" is a synonym for "envision," so readers can infer that "imagine" is a synonym as well.

5. A chocolatier is a person who makes chocolate. The passage states, "To transform these bitter cocoa beans into delicious chocolate, chocolatiers have to first dry out the beans." This suggests that the chocolatier is the person who takes the cocoa beans and makes them into chocolate.

6. **C.** In this sentence, "the finished product" refers to the chocolate. The cocoa beans and cocoa nibs occur earlier in the process. The very next sentence starts with the words, "The chocolate," which shows us that the author used the phrase "the finished product" to refer to the chocolate. Later, a candy bar is introduced as one treat that can be made with the chocolate.

7. **B.** The cocoa liquor and cocoa butter are removed from the cocoa nibs.

8. **A** and **C.** The chocolate bar travels from one place to another to get to the consumer, and it also undergoes a long process as it is transformed from cocoa beans into chocolate. "A fun trip or vacation" or 'ocean voyage' doesn't make sense in this context, and although "hard work" is required to make the chocolate, it's NOT a definition for the word "journey."

RI.2.5 Use Text Features & Search Tools

1. **C.** Headings are intended to help readers find the main idea of sections in order to locate information easily.

2. **B.** Bold text is used to indicate key words and phrases and draw the reader's attention to this essential information.

3. **D.** This section contains information about rock features, including stalactites, which are rock formationss that hang from the ceiling.

4. **B.** Bats are cave creatures, which are discussed under the heading "Cave Creatures."

5. **A.** Paragraphs. The key difference between solutional caves and sea caves is provided in paragraphs (Paragraphs 4 and 5), including the facts that, solutional caves are formed by rainfall and chemical processes, while sea caves are formed by erosion.

6. Part A- **D.** The article explains that sea caves form when sea cliffs are eroded by waves and tides.

Part B- **B** and **C.** Readers could immediately go to the heading "Types of Caves" to find information about sea caves. They could then quickly locate the definition using the bolded text.

7. **D.** Searching "Cave types" would lead to information about all the different kinds of caves. Searching "Solutional caves" would only provide information on one type of cave rather than on many different types.

8. **A.** A glossary is an alphabetical list of words with definitions.

RI.2.6 Identify Point Of View of Self & Author

1. **1st and 3rd Choices.** These sentences best express the author's overall point of view: that exercise offers many excellent benefits. The other two options are specific details that support this viewpoint.

2. Part A - **C.** The author might agree with options A and B, but we don't know this information based on the text. D is incorrect because the author points out that you don't have to go to the gym to experience the benefits of exercise.

Part B- **D.** This piece of evidence includes information about exercise benefitting both the body and the mind.

3. Answers will vary. Correct answers will include an explanation of why students agree or disagree with the viewpoint stated in the article (that exercising is beneficial and important). They will state specific details from the passage and explain how they influenced the student's point of view (to agree or disagree with the author's viewpoint) Example:" I agree with the viewpoint that exercise is important for your body and mind. When you exercise, you can maintain a healthy body weight and at the same time, you will feel happier and more relaxed. It also helps prevent diseases that harm your health, like diabetes." The passage contains less evidence to use if a student disagrees with the author.

4. **C.** The author's point of view is that too much TV is harmful. The other details are included in the article, but they're too specific and don't represent the author's overall viewpoint.

5. **A.** "Don't overdo it," best summarizes the author's point of view about television. The other words don't give us enough information to express the author's viewpoint.

6. Part A- **C.** A is incorrect because the author believes TV is fine in moderation. B is never mentioned in the passage. D is too much of a generalization. The author does say that kids who witness bad behaviors on TV may imitate it, but does not claim that all kids who watch TV behave badly.

Part B- **B.** This quote shows that the author believes activities like reading and spending time with family are healthier than watching television.

7. Answers ma vary. Correct answers will state whether the student agrees or disagrees with the author's viewpoint (that too much television harms children) and explain the reasoning behind this stance. Student reasoning for whether they agree or disagree must be supported with information from the passage. For this reason, it makes it difficult for students to disagree with the author's viewpoint. The passage is filled with facts supporting why children need to watch less television. A typical child will likely disagree with the article because they like to watch television or because they disagree that watching television is unhealthy or can lead to violent behavior. However, these are opinions based on the student's thinking and not based on the facts from the article.

8. The title of the article is "Turn Off the TV." Immediately, readers understand that the author may think television (or too much television) is bad, since the author is encouraging people to stop watching.

RI.3.7 Use & Understand Information In Illustrations

1. **A.** The passage explains that gas molecules are spread out, and the image also shows that they are by far the most spread out molecules among the states of matter.

2. **C.** The illustration helps readers visualize the information that is provided in the text, and, in this case, also adds new information (with the arrows and labels) about the ways that states of matter change.

3. **C.** The shape of a solid does not change, even if it's placed in a container.

4. Liquid, Solid. The arrow and "Freezing" label on the image indicates that a liquid can change into a solid through the process of freezing.

5. Based on the illustration, it looks like a liquid can turn into a gas. There are arrows pointing from the liquid to the gas with the label "evaporation".

6. **1st and 3rd Choices.** Gas and liquid molecules move around, but solid molecules don't. Condensation is not a type of molecule.

7. **B.** Europa is the only one of Jupiter's four largest moons that is not larger than Earth's moon.

8. **D.** Saturn's moon Titan is much larger than

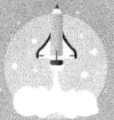

Earth's moon. Neptune's moon Triton looks close in size to Earth's moon, but Titan is much bigger, making Saturn the better answer.

RI.3.8 Describe & Make Connections In Text

1. **B.** The information in Paragraph 2 introduces the reader to Bethany's passion for surfing. The author states that "Bethany was home schooled so that she could pursue her passion for surfing." It also describes how Bethany is able to beat people who have surfed longer than her, so we can infer that she works hard and really enjoys surfing.

2. **B.** Paragraph 3 introduces the cause which is Bethany is attacked by the shark. Paragraph 4 introduces the effects of shark attack such as: she has to go to the hospital, she loses a lot of blood, she loses her arm, and she has to have a lot of surgeries.

3. Paragraph 5 shows us that Bethany did not stop surfing just because she lost her arm. It also shows us that Bethany refused to give up. Students may include any of the following details to support their answer: "Despite losing her arm, Bethany pledged to get back to surfing as soon as possible." Also, just one month after the attack, Bethany returned to surfing. Lastly, she continued to be a great surfer with one arm because she won awards and competitions.

4. **2nd, 3rd, 5th & 6th Choices.** Students should select the following answer choices: Bethany undergoes many surgeries, Bethany loses her arm, Bethany loses a lot of blood, and Bethany makes a promise to herself to return to surfing. The 4th answer choice, Bethany has to stay in the hospital for several months, is incorrect because the passage states that Bethany is released from the hospital a few days later.

5. **D.** In Paragraph 3, we learn that school is very hard for Patricia. We learn that she tried to learn how to read and write, but she just couldn't do it. There are no clues in this paragraph that Patricia is a bad student or that she could have tried harder. It is not interesting background information about Patricia because it is important for the reader to understand that Patricia still couldn't read or write, despite trying very hard in school.

6. **A.** In Paragraph 1, we are introduced to Patricia and her family. In Paragraph 2, we learn more about Patricia and her family. We learn that her parents get divorced, and we learn that Patricia has to live in two separate places. There is no cause/effect or problem/solution relationship between Paragraph 1 and Paragraph 2.

7. Answers may vary. Several factors have helped Patricia to become a famous author. In Paragraph 5, we learn that she is diagnosed with dyslexia and finally gets the help she needs. Therefore, Patricia learns how to read. In Paragraph 6, the author explains that Patricia is a wonderful example of what can happen if we work hard and never give up. Students may also include that Patricia still went to school and worked hard even though she was bullied. Students should include any 2 of these reasons.

8. **B.** Paragraph 4 gives us some insight into the bullying that Patricia encountered. As a result, we know that she started to hate school because the author states: "Eventually, she despised going to school." While students may be tempted to selected Letter D, the focus of this paragraph is not to describe why bullying is bad. Furthermore, the paragraph does not describe the full effects that bullying has on Patricia other than she despised going to school.

RI.3.9. Compare And Contrast Key Points In Two Texts

1. **C.** Both passages acknowledge that cell phones may distract students from learning.

2. **D.** The author of Passage 1 thinks that students shouldn't be allowed to have phones at school at all, while the author of Passage 2 thinks students should be able to have phones at school and simply not allowed to take them out in class.

3. The author of Passage 1 thinks cell phones shouldn't be allowed in school at all, and Passage 1 only addresses bad aspects of cell phone usage. Passage 2 addresses both sides of the issue and explain some reasons that cell

phones may be good to have at school.

4. **A.** Passage 1 mentions that students may use cell phones to share answers on assignments and tests. The rest of the answer choices are mentioned in both passages, although they may not be stated in the exact words as the answer choices.

5. **1st & 4th answer choices**: (1): Students may need to contact parents in case of emergency.(4) Students and parents may need to contact one another if plans related to transportation or pick up times change.

6. **C.** The author of Passage 2 would likely say that rules about students not having cell phones in class must be enforced, or that students must be responsible enough not to use cell phones in class. However, she would argue that students do need to have cell phones at school for safety reasons and to be able to contact parents as needed (and vice versa).

7. Responses may vary. Correct answers will take a position for Passage 1 or for Passage 2 and will mention key arguments from the passage that the student found convincing.

An example of a student explanation who agrees with Passage 1 may state: I agree with Passage 1 the most. I agree with Passage 1 because cell phones do cause too much temptation. If you are too busy looking at your phone or even thinking about your phone, you are missing important information from the teacher.

An example of a student explanation who agrees with Passage 2 may state: I agree with Passage 2 the most. I agree with Passage 2 because I think students need to have them in case of an emergency. Students should be responsible enough to keep their cell phones in their backpacks during school time so that they do not get distracted.

8. **B.** Learning. Both passages mention that school is about learning and that cell phones should not interrupt the learning process.

LANGUAGE

L.1.1 Demonstrate Command of Grammar & Usage

1. **A.** Adjectives are used to describe or clarify nouns by giving more information about their size, color, shape, age, material, etc.

2. **C.** The word *large* describes the noun dog, giving readers more information about its size.

3. **B.** The word *he* is a pronoun used to replace the antecedent *Mr. White.*

4. **B.** The comparative adjective *bigger* correctly completes this sentence, which compares the size of the horse to the size of the dog. -Er is added to the end of adjectives when they adjective is used to compare two nouns.

5. **D.** The plural form of the noun *bus* is the plural noun buses, so we must add an -es to the end of the word.

6. **B.** *Walked* agrees with the first-person subject I and the tense (past). This sentence is in past tense because of the word *yesterday.*

7. **A.** *Sing* correctly completes this sentence. *Sang* and *sung* are past tense, while *singing* is present tense. When combined with *will, sing* is future tense and agrees with the first-person plural subject *we.*

8. **C.** *Their* agrees with the antecedent *Michael and Jose.*

9. **B.** The speaker of the sentence wants to both go to Disney World and bring her best friends, requiring the coordinating conjunction *and.* The two sentences do not contrast, so we can't use *but* or *yet,* and *nor* is used for negative possibilities.

10. **D.** It makes sense for John to go to soccer practice *after* school. Additionally, none of the other possible options form grammatically correct sentences.

11. **B.** This sentence contains two independent clauses, so it is compound. An independent clause is a clause that can stand by itself as a sentence.

12. **C.** This sentence is complex because it contains both a dependent clause and an independent clause. A dependent clause is a clause that cannot stand by itself as a sentence.

L.1.2 Know Capitalization, Punctuation & Spelling

1. **C.** In titles, it is necessary to capitalize the first

   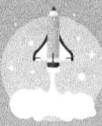      

and last word, in addition to nouns, pronouns, verbs, and adjectives. In this title, *Lion*, *Witch*, and *Wardrobe* need to be capitalized. *The* must also be capitalized because it is the first word in the sentence, but any additional appearance of *the* must be lowercase. The word *and* is not capitalized because it is a conjunction.

2. **D.** When an address is written as a line of text, commas must separate the street, state, and city. Commas are not needed between words and numbers, such as the building number or the zip code.

3. **A.** Quotation marks must go only around dialogue, and the comma should be placed before the closing quotation marks.

4. **C.** This sentence correctly puts quotation marks only around dialogue. There is a comma before the closing quotation marks and between the word *said* and the additional dialogue.

5. **B.** The apostrophe *s* indicates possession, showing that the car belongs to the man.

6. **C.** With a plural noun, like teachers, the possessive apostrophe comes after the *s* instead of before. This is to indicate that the noun is both plural and possessive.

7. **A.** *Cries* is the correct spelling for the present tense form of *cry*. Cry ends with a *-y* so the *-y* is replaced by an *-i* before adding the *-es* ending.

8. **D.** The suffix *-ed* indicates that a verb is past tense.

9. **C.** The suffix *-ing* indicates that a verb is present tense.

10. **A.** The suffix *-ness* means "the state of" something. In this case, *happiness* is the correct word to refer to the state of being happy.

L.2.3 Use Appropriate Language Conventions

1. **D.** Alexis was sad throughout the day because she thought everyone forgot her birthday. Before Alexis goes into the house, she thinks about how she wants to go to sleep and forget "the worst birthday ever." Based on this information, readers know that Alexis was surprised when she saw all of her friends, family, cake, and presents.

2. **B.** The characteristics listed are not common, making the starfish unique. Additionally, the phrase "unlike most animals" also hints that the correct answer is "unique."

3. **B.** The fact that the villagers had nightmares for weeks indicates that they feel terrified. *Nervous* is not strong enough to describe the way people would feel about a giant fire-breathing dragon.

4. **A.** The first blank is contrasted with what Michael Jordan could have done after not making the team (given up and decided he would never be a great basketball player). This suggests that he used not making the team as motivation. The second blank indicates that the correct word is something that can keep a person going, also showing that motivation is the correct answer.

5. **C.** The girl would feel sad about her ice cream falling on the ground. The usage of "fell" also shows that this was an accident that was not meant to happen, so readers can infer the girl felt sad about it.

6. **B.** This sentence is not a good description of the ocean. Choices A, C and D offer facts about the ocean. Choice B states an opinion that is relevant to one person.

7. **D.** This answer choice best describes a happy puppy. Choices A and C describe behaviors we would more likely see from a sad or angry puppy. Choice B doesn't necessarily indicate that the puppy is happy, so it's not a good description.

8. **A.** "You crack me up," means that someone is funny and makes you laugh.

9. **C.** Going the extra mile has nothing to do with physical distances or running. It simply means going above and beyond what is expected or required.

10. **D.** Being "under the weather" means being sick. It's also the most logical answer choice listed.

L.3.4 Determine Meaning of Unknown Word/s in Context

1. **C.** Based on the examples of *fish*, *whales*, and *dolphins*, we can determine that the word **aquatic** is related to water. From the answer

choices provided, water is the only option that all three examples have in common.

2. **A.** The definition of the word **sterilize** appears in the sentence when it's explained that the reason Mom sterilized the bottle was to "make sure it was clean."

3. An example of a student explanation: **Pewter** means gray. Both elephants and hippos have gray skin. The word *color* is another context clue in this sentence.

4. **C.** Because the waitress was in a bad mood, we can infer that she was not very polite to the customers.

5. **B.** This sentence indicates that the word **adept** must contrast with the word *terrible*. We know this because Jimmy was terrible at crossword puzzles, *but* his sister was very adept at them.

6. **D.** If agree means to share the same opinion about something, agreeable must mean that people are capable of/able to share an opinion on a topic.

7. Incomplete means not finished. The prefix *in* means *in, on,* or *not*. In this context, the only definition that makes sense is "not complete."

8. Preheat means to heat before, while reheat means to heat again. The prefix *pre* means *prior to, before, in advance of,* or *early,* and the prefix *re* means *back* or *again*.

9. Each of these words share the root word **sect**. The root word **sect** means cut. The prefix **bi** means twice or two. **Bisect** means to cut in two.

10. **A.** To use the word *happy* as a noun, the state of being happy, you need to use the suffix -ness. The suffix -ly transforms *happy* into an adverb. The suffixes -ing and -ed cannot be used because they would not transform *happy* into real words.

L.3.5 Understand Word Relationships and Nuances in Meaning

1. **B.** In this sentence, the phrase *take steps* is used figuratively to mean take action or do something about it. Literal walking or running probably won't fix Chloe's relationship with her friend Naya, but taking action will.

2. **A.** This is another example of figurative language. When the sentence says that Max has *the upper hand,* it means he has the advantage over his brother. His hand being on top or being bigger is not relevant to the context of the sentence, which describes a wrestling competition. We can infer that Max has the advantage, and not the disadvantage, because he is bigger and stronger than his brother.

3. The sentence is figurative. Sarah could not literally eat a horse (and probably wouldn't want to either). This is hyperbole (exaggerated for effect), and meant to express that Sarah is extremely hungry. An example of an appropriate student explanation may state: This sentence is figurative. I know this because Sarah could not actually eat a horse. The phrase *could eat a horse* is used to show that someone is very hungry.

4. The sentence is figurative. The boy is not literally as tall as a giraffe. This is a simile meant to express that the boy is very tall. An example of an appropriate student explanation may state: This sentence is figurative. I know this because it is not possible for the boy to actually be as tall as a giraffe. The phrase *as tall as a giraffe* is used to show that someone is incredibly tall.

5. **B.** *Aggravated* is similar in meaning to *annoyed*. *Amused* and *joyful* are both positive words, while *annoyed* is negative. *Confused* is not relevant or close in meaning to *annoyed*.

6. **C.** *Massive* means large, so *huge* is similar in meaning. It does not refer specifically to height or length, so *short* and *long* are incorrect. *Tiny* is an antonym for *massive,* not a synonym.

7. **D.** *Fascinated* means interested or awestruck, so *bored* has the opposite meaning. *Entertained* is very close in meaning to *fascinated,* while *happy* and *scared* aren't related.

8. **B.** The word *skipped* implies that the boy was happy on his walk home, as mentioned in the sentence. *Stomped* has an angry connotation, while there's nothing in the sentence to suggest that *ran* or *tiptoed* would be a more accurate description.

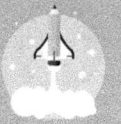

9. **B.** *Furious* is a much stronger word than *mad, displeased* or *irritated.* Choice B is more powerful and implies that Anthony is more upset. An example of an appropriate student explanation may state: Furious shows that Anthony is the most upset. I know this because the words *mad, displeased,* and *irritated* do not show that Anthony is very upset.

10. **C.** Laughing is the only positive word among these choices. Frowning and smirking all have somewhat negative connotations. Staring is not related.

11. **A.** If students don't know the meaning of the word *sluggish,* it can still be inferred that *slow* is a synonym, since the turtle finished the race last. *Speedy* and *fast* wouldn't make sense in this context, and *friendly* is irrelevant to the sentence.

L.3.6 Know Academic/ Domain-Specific Words

1. **B.** A simile is a type of figurative language that students would learn about in English/Language Arts class.

2. **C.** The total amount when adding two or more numbers is a sum.

3. **D.** Amphibians are a class of animal that students would learn about in Science.

4. **C.** Using context clues means using the known words and phrases in a sentence to determine the meaning of the unknown word.

5. **B.** Antecedents are the nouns replaced by pronouns, and students would learn this term in English/Language Arts class.

6. **B.** Contrast means to describe the differences between two or more items.

7. **A.** The Solar System refers to the planets and moons that orbit the sun. Choice B describes the digestive system, Choice C describes the water cycle, and Choice D describes cloud types.

8. **B.** The phrase "stepping on the back of my shoes" indicates that the student is behind the writer. Additionally, the fact that the students are in line indicates "to the right of" and "next to" are most likely incorrect answers.

9. **D.** We can infer that the correct answer is "before" because the sentence includes the phrase "wake up early enough."

10. **B.** The use of the phrase "my head," in addition to knowledge about the location of an airplane, indicates that the correct answer is "above."

PARCC
PRACTICE TEST

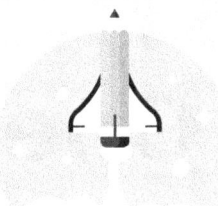

PARCC

Grade 3
ELA/Literacy
Practice Test One

Unit 1
(Literary Analysis)

Directions: Read the passage "The Country Mouse and the City Mouse" and then answer Numbers 1 through 3.

Passage 1: The Country Mouse and the City Mouse

1   Once a little mouse who lived in the country invited a little Mouse from the city to visit him. When the little City Mouse sat down to dinner he was surprised to find that the Country Mouse had nothing to eat except barley and grain.

2   "Really," he said, "you do not live well at all; you should see how I live! I have all sorts of fine things to eat every day. You must come to visit me and see how nice it is to live in the city."

3   The little Country Mouse was glad to do this, and after a while he went to the city to visit his friend.

4   The very first place that the City Mouse took the Country Mouse to see was the kitchen cupboard of the house where he lived. There, on the lowest shelf, behind some stone jars, stood a big paper bag of brown sugar. The little City Mouse gnawed a hole in the bag and invited his friend to nibble for himself.

5   The two little mice nibbled and nibbled, and the Country Mouse thought he had never tasted anything so delicious in his life. He was just thinking how lucky the City Mouse was, when suddenly the door opened with a bang, and in came the cook to get some flour.

6   "Run!" whispered the City Mouse. And they ran as fast as they could to the little hole where they had come in. The little Country Mouse was shaking all over when they got safely away, but the little City Mouse said, "That is nothing; she will soon go away and then we can go back."

7   "This is very terrible," said the little Country Mouse; "let us not go back to the cupboard again."

8   "No," said the City Mouse, "I will take you to the cellar; there is something special there."

9   So the City Mouse took his little friend down the cellar stairs and into a big cupboard where there were many shelves. On the shelves were jars of butter, and cheeses in bags and out of bags. Overhead hung bunches of sausages, and there were spicy apples in barrels standing about. It smelled so good that it went to the little Country Mouse's head. He ran along the shelf and nibbled at a cheese here, and a bit of butter there, until he saw an especially rich, very delicious-smelling piece of cheese on a queer little stand in a corner. He was just on the point of putting his teeth into the cheese when the City Mouse saw him.

10   "Stop! stop!" cried the City Mouse. "That is a trap!"

11 The little Country Mouse stopped and said, "What is a trap?"

12 "That thing is a trap," said the little City Mouse. "The minute you touch the cheese with your teeth something comes down on your head hard, and you won't survive."

13 The little Country Mouse looked at the trap, and he looked at the cheese, and he looked at the little City Mouse. "If you'll excuse me," he said, "I think I will go home. I'd rather have barley and grain to eat and eat it in peace and comfort, than have brown sugar and dried prunes and cheese,—and be frightened to death all the time!"

14 So the little Country Mouse went back to his home, and there he stayed all the rest of his life.

Now answer Numbers 1 through 3. Base your answers on the passage "The Country Mouse and the City Mouse."

1. Based on the information in the passage "The Country Mouse and the City Mouse", complete at least 5 empty boxes in this table. For the Country Mouse, what is good and bad about living in the city? What is good and bad about living in the country?

Good things about the city	Bad things about the city	Good things about the country	Bad things about the country
Brown sugar	People chasing the mice		
Dried prunes			

2. This question has two parts. First, answer Part A. Then, answer Part B.

Part A

What life lesson does the Country Mouse learn in the passage "The Country Mouse and the City Mouse"?

   A. Treat others how you want to be treated.
   B. Be happy with what you have.
   C. We can't trust everyone.
   D. Country life is always better than city life.

Part B

Select the piece of evidence from the passage that best supports your answer in Part A.
- A. "'If you'll excuse me,' he said, 'I think I will go home. I'd rather have barley and grain to eat and eat it in peace and comfort, than have brown sugar and dried prunes and cheese,—and be frightened to death all the time!'" (Paragraph 13)
- B. "The two little mice nibbled and nibbled, and the Country Mouse thought he had never tasted anything so delicious in his life." (Paragraph 5)
- C. "He was just thinking how lucky the City Mouse was, when suddenly the door opened with a bang, and in came the cook to get some flour." (Paragraph 5)
- D. "When the little City Mouse sat down to dinner he was surprised to find that the Country Mouse had nothing to eat except barley and grain. 'Really,' he said, 'you do not live well at all; you should see how I live! I have all sorts of fine things to eat every day.'" (Paragraph 1-2)

3. This question has two parts. First, answer Part A. Then, answer Part B.

Part A

What does 'gnawed' mean as it is used in paragraph 4 of the passage "The Country Mouse and the City Mouse"?
- A. Chewed
- B. Cut
- C. Tore
- D. Made

Part B

Which phrase from the passage helps the reader understand the meaning of the word 'gnawed'?
- A. "...a big paper bag of brown sugar" (paragraph 4)
- B. "...Country Mouse thought he had never tasted anything so delicious in his life" (paragraph 5)
- C. "That thing is a trap," (paragraph 12)
- D. "...invited his friend to nibble for himself" (paragraph 4)

Directions: Read the passage "The Boy Who Cried Wolf" then answer Numbers 4 through 6.

Passage 2: The Boy Who Cried Wolf

1   There was once a shepherd-boy who kept his flock at a little distance from the village. Once he thought he would play a trick on the villagers and have some fun at their expense. So he ran toward the village crying out, with all his might,—

2   "Wolf! Wolf! Come and help! The wolves are at my lambs!"

3   The kind villagers left their work and ran to the field to help him. But when they got there the boy laughed at them for their pains; there was no wolf there.

4   Still another day the boy tried the same trick, and the villagers came running to help and got laughed at again. Then one day a wolf did break into the fold and began attacking the lambs. In great fright, the boy ran for help. "Wolf! Wolf!" he screamed. "There is a wolf in the flock! Help!"

5   The villagers heard him, but they thought it was another mean trick; no one paid the least attention, or went near him. And the shepherd-boy lost all his sheep.

Now answer Numbers 4 through 6. Base your answers on the passages "The Boy Who Cried Wolf" and "The City and the Country Mouse".

4. This question has two parts. First, answer Part A. Then, answer Part B.

Part A
Why does the boy yell that there's a wolf the first two times in the passage "The Boy Who Cried Wolf"?
- **A.** There really is a wolf.
- **B.** He thinks it will be fun to trick the villagers.
- **C.** He's a mean boy who wants to upset and be unkind to the villagers.
- **D.** He's bored and looking for something to do.

Part B
Choose one detail from the passage "The Boy Who Cried Wolf" that best supports the answer in Part A.
- **A.** "…one day a wolf did break into the fold and began attacking the lambs." (paragraph 4)
- **B.** "The villagers heard him, but they thought it was another mean trick;" (paragraph 5)
- **C.** "…he thought he would play a trick on the villagers and have some fun at their expense." (paragraph 1)
- **D.** "In great fright, the boy ran for help. "Wolf! Wolf!" he screamed." (paragraph 4)

5. This question has two parts. First, answer Part A. Then, answer Part B.

Part A

Which of the following words best describes the villagers at the beginning of the passage "The Boy Who Cried Wolf"?

    A. Busy
    B. Untrusting
    C. Caring
    D. Mean

Part B

Which statement from the passage best supports the answer in Part A?

    A. "....no one paid the least attention, or went near him." (paragraph 5)
    B. "In great fright, the boy ran for help." (paragraph 4)
    C. "...villagers left their work and ran to the field to help him." (paragraph 3)
    D. "...the boy laughed at them for their pains."(paragraph 3)

6. Which of the following are similarities between the two passages?
Choose **ALL** that apply.
    ☐ They teach a lesson.
    ☐ They include both animals and people.
    ☐ They are both written in the third person point of view.
    ☐ They both teach readers to be grateful for what they have.
    ☐ The both teach readers that they should not lie.

7. You have read two passages describing characters who learn a life lesson. Write an essay that explains the lessons learned by one or more of the characters in the story. Use evidence from the passage or passages (including the characters' words and actions) to support your answer.

Directions: Read the passage "The Little Doll" and then answer Numbers 8 through 11.

Passage 3: The Little Doll
by Charles Kingsley

1. I once had a sweet little doll, dears,
   The prettiest doll in the world;
   Her cheeks were so red and so white; dears,
   And her hair was so charmingly curled.

2. But I lost my poor little doll, dears,
   As I played in the heath one day;
   And I cried for her more than a week, dears;
   But I never could find where she lay.

3. I found my poor little doll, dears,
   As I played in the heath one day:
   Folks say she is terrible changed, dears,
   For her paint is all washed away,
   And her arm trodden off by the cows, dears,
   And her hair not the least bit curled:
   Yet for old sakes' sake she is still, dears,
   The prettiest doll in the world.

Now answer Numbers 8 through 11. Base your answers on the passages "The Little Doll".

8. This question has two parts. First, answer Part A. Then, answer Part B.

Part A

What is the speaker's point of view in this poem?
- **A.** First person
- **B.** Second person
- **C.** Third person
- **D.** Third person limited

Part B

Which sentence best supports the answer in Part A?
- **A.** "And her hair not the least bit curled."
- **B.** "Folks say she is terrible changed..."
- **C.** "Yet for old sakes' sake she is still..."
- **D.** "I once had a sweet little doll..."

9. Complete the following sequence of events from the poem.
    (1) The child owns a beautiful doll.
    (2) ?
    (3) The child cries about the lost doll for more than a week.
    (4) The child finds the doll.
    (5) ?

    A. (2) The child loses the doll; (5) The doll is ruined, and the child gives her away.
    B. (2) Someone takes the child's doll; (5) The doll looks just the same as before.
    C. (2) The child loses the doll; (5) The doll is changed, but the child still loves her.
    D. (2) Someone takes the child's doll; (5) The child is upset that her doll has changed.

10. Complete the table below to describe the doll's appearance at the beginning of the poem and the doll's appearance at the end of the poem.

Doll's Appearance at the Beginning of the Poem	Doll's Appearance at the End of the Poem
Hair charmingly curled	Hair not least bit curled

11. This question has two parts. First, answer Part A. Then, answer Part B.

Part A
Which of the following is a life lesson that readers can learn from this poem?

    A. Never play in the heath.
    B. Appearance doesn't matter.
    C. You can't trust everyone.
    D. Don't take your toys outside.

Part B
Which line from the poem supports your answer to Part A?
    A. "But I lost my poor little doll, dears, As I played in the heath one day…"
    B. "Folks say she is terrible changed, dears, For her paint is all washed away…"
    C. "And I cried for her more than a week, dears; But I never could find where she lay."
    D. "Yet for old sakes' sake she is still, dears, The prettiest doll in the world."

PARCC

Grade 3 ELA/Literacy Practice Test One

Unit 2 (Research Simulation Task)

Directions: Read the passage "Hummingbird" and then answer Numbers 12 through 13.

Passage 4: Hummingbirds

1   If you've ever been close to a hummingbird, you've probably heard the buzzing noise they make when they fly. Hummingbirds make this noise because of how quickly they can flap their wings. They can beat their wings as many as 80 times in a single second! This gives them the ability to hover in the air, like a helicopter. Hummingbirds are also the only bird that flies backwards.

2   Moving so fast requires a lot of energy. This means that hummingbirds need to eat more than you would expect for such a small bird. Their favorite food is nectar, a sweet liquid that can be found inside flowers. Hummingbirds have to visit hundreds of flowers to get enough nectar each day. Every day, they drink more than their body weight in nectar.

3   It looks like hummingbirds use their long beaks like straws, but they really use their tongues to drink nectar. They lap up nectar from flowers the same way your dog or cat might lap up water from a bowl.

4   Flowers feed hummingbirds and help them gain energy, but hummingbirds help flowers too. When hummingbirds drink nectar, they get pollen from the flowers on their heads and beaks. Pollen is what helps flowers make seeds.

5   As the hummingbirds fly to more flowers to drink more nectar, they also spread pollen and help flowers make more seeds. Then more flowers grow, and the hummingbird has even more nectar to drink!

Now answer Numbers 12 through 13. Base your answers on the passage "Hummingbird".

12. This question has two parts. First, answer Part A. Then, answer Part B.

Part A
According to the passage "Hummingbird", why do hummingbirds require so much energy?
- **A.** They need energy to fly for long distances.
- **B.** They are large birds who need plenty of energy.
- **C.** They are small birds who need enough energy to fight off larger predators.
- **D.** They need energy because they move so quickly.

Part B
Which detail from the passage **best** supports the answer in Part A?
- **A.** "Hummingbirds have to visit hundreds of flowers to get enough nectar each day."(paragraph 2)
- **B.** "...hummingbirds need to eat more than you would expect for such a small bird." (paragraph 2)
- **C.** "They can beat their wings as many as 80 times in a single second!" (paragraph 1)
- **D.** "...they really use their tongues to drink nectar." (paragraph 3)

13. Which statement BEST describes the relationship between hummingbirds and flowers?
- **A.** Flowers help hummingbirds by giving them food and energy.
- **B.** Hummingbirds help flowers by spreading their seeds.
- **C.** Hummingbirds and flowers have a mutually helpful relationship.
- **D.** Hummingbirds eat the nectar from flowers.

Directions: Read the passage "Honey Badgers" then answer Numbers 14 through 18.

Passage 5: Honey Badgers

1   Honey badgers aren't very big, but they sure are tough. They're only a couple feet long and weigh just over 20 pounds, but they've been known to chase away lions. After they chase away the lions, they take the food the lions have hunted and eat it for themselves instead.

2   How can such a tiny animal be so tough? The honey badger is equipped with helpful weapons. For example, honey badgers have extremely thick skin. Arrows, bites from other animals, and even small bullets can't pierce the honey badgers' tough skin. Honey badger's teeth are strong too. A honey badger can bite through a turtle shell.

3   Honey badgers also have long, sharp claws. The claws are great for fighting off predators, but they're also useful for digging. Honey badgers can dig a nine-foot tunnel in just 10 minutes. They use this ability to construct their homes, which are small tunnels in the ground. If any predator approaches the honey badger's home, even a cow or a horse, the honey badgers will attack fiercely to defend their territory.

4   If honey badgers are so ferocious, why do they have such a "sweet" name? Well, honey badgers love to eat honey. Because their skin is so tough, they can invade beehives without being injured with bee stings. Beekeepers in Africa have to use electric fences to keep honey badgers from eating all of the honey their bees produce.

Now answer Numbers 14 through 17. Base your answers on the passages "Hummingbird" and "Honey Badgers".

14. According to the passage "Honey Badgers", which of the following are NOT helpful weapons for honey badgers? Choose the TWO details that apply.
    - [ ] Strong teeth
    - [ ] Sharp spikes
    - [ ] Sharp claws
    - [ ] Tough skin
    - [ ] Long furry tail

15. This question has two parts. First, answer Part A. Then, answer Part B.

Part A

What is the main idea of the passage "Honey Badgers"?
A. Honey badgers are both sweet and vicious.
B. Honey badgers are much tougher than they look.
C. Honey badgers are dangerous for bees.
D. Honey badgers can scare off lions.

Part B
Which detail from the passage **best** supports the answer to Part A?
- A. "They're only a couple feet long and weigh just over 20 pounds." (paragraph 1)
- B. "The honey badger is equipped with helpful weapons." (paragraph 2)
- C. "...honey badgers love to eat honey." (paragraph 4)
- D. "... they take the food the lions have hunted and eat it for themselves" (paragraph 4)

16. This question has two parts. First, answer Part A. Then, answer Part B.

Part A
With which statement would the author of the passage "Honey Badgers" most likely agree?
- A. Honey badgers can successfully fight or scare off much bigger predators.
- B. Honey badgers should have a different name, because they aren't sweet like their name suggests.
- C. Beekeepers shouldn't build electric fences to keep out honey badgers.
- D. Honey badgers are at a disadvantage with other predators because of their small size.

Part B
Select the piece of evidence from the text that **best** supports your answer in Part A.
- A. "The claws are great for fighting off predators, but they're also useful for digging. Honey badgers can dig a nine-foot tunnel in just 10 minutes." (Paragraph 3)
- B. "If any predator approaches the honey badger's home, even a cow or a horse, the honey badgers will attack fiercely to defend their territory." (Paragraph 3)
- C. "If honey badgers are so ferocious, why do they have such a "sweet" name? Well, honey badgers love to eat honey." (Paragraph 4)
- D. "Beekeepers in Africa have to use electric fences to keep honey badgers from eating all of the honey their bees produce." (Paragraph 4)

17. What do the illustrations in both the "Hummingbird" and "Honey Badgers" passages add to these passages?
- A. They provide a lot more information about hummingbirds and honey badgers.
- B. They brighten up the passages and entertain the readers.
- C. They help readers visualize and understand the information about hummingbirds and honey badgers from the passages.
- D. They emphasize that both hummingbirds and honey badgers are beautiful, unique creatures.

18. The passages describe how the hummingbird and honey badger have unusual features and how these features help them and affect the environment.

Write an article for a nature magazine about these two unique creatures. In your article, describe the special features of the hummingbird and honey badger, and the benefits and/or drawbacks of these features for the animals and their environments. Which creature, in your opinion, is most helpful to its environment?
Use specific details and examples from the passages to support your ideas.

PARCC

Grade 3 ELA/Literacy Practice Test One

Unit 2 (Research Simulation Task)

Directions: Read the passage "The Fisherman and His Wife" and answer Numbers 19 through 22.

Passage 6: The Fisherman and His Wife

1   Once upon a time a fisherman who lived with his wife in a little, old shack close by the sea, and every day he went out fishing.

2   One day, he caught a flounder. The flounder said to him, "Please fisherman, let me live! I'm not really a flounder, but an enchanted prince."

3   The fisherman let the magic fish go, and then he went home to his wife in the little, old shack.

4   "Husband," said his wife, "You didn't catch any fish today?"

5   "I did catch a flounder," said the man. "But he said he was really an enchanted prince, so I let him go."

6   "You didn't wish for anything?" said his wife. "It's hard to always live in this disgusting, smelly, old shack.. Go back and call the fish. Tell him we want to have a new hut, he will surely give us that."

7   The man went back to the sea and called to the magic fish. "My wife says I should have made a wish," he told the fish. "She wants a new hut."

8   "Go home," said the flounder. "She has her wish already."

9   When the man went home, a new hut had replaced the dirty, old, shack. His wife showed him how much better the hut was, and they were very happy.

10   About two weeks later, the man's wife decided the hut was too small. This time, his wife wished for a great stone castle. The fish granted her wish again. But she still wasn't satisfied.

11   Next, the wife wished that she and her husband could be king and queen. The flounder obliged the wife again. She was happy, but not for long. No matter what wishes the flounder granted, the wife always wanted more.

12   Finally, she told her husband, "Just tell the fish to give me everything I deserve."

13   The man told the flounder about his wife's wish, and the flounder said, "Go home, her wish has already been granted."

14   When the man returned home, he found his wife crying. The stone castle had been transformed back into a little, old shack.

Now answer Numbers 19 through 22. Base your answers on the passage "The Fisherman and His Wife".

19. This question has two parts. First, answer Part A. Then, answer Part B.

Part A

What life lesson can readers learn from this story?
- **A.** Never ask for anything.
- **B.** Be grateful for what you have.
- **C.** Don't talk to strangers.
- **D.** Be kind to others.

Part B

Which of the following details from the story best supports your answer in Part A?
- **A.** "'I did catch a flounder,'" said the man. "'But he said he was really an enchanted prince, so I let him go.'" (paragraph 5)
- **B.** "When the man went home, a small hut had replaced the dirty, old shack. His wife showed him how much better the hut was, and they were very happy." (paragraph 9)
- **C.** "No matter what wishes the flounder granted, the wife always wanted more." (paragraph 11)
- **D.** "Next, the wife wished that she and her husband could be king and queen. The flounder granted her wish again." (paragraph 11)

20. Select the event that correctly completes this sequence of events from the passage.
    (1) The man catches a flounder.
    (2) The man lets go of the flounder, who is an enchanted prince.
    (3) The man's wife tells him to go back and wish for a new hut instead of an old shack, and the fish grants the wish.
    (4) The wife asks for a stone castle, and the fish grants the wish.
    (5) The wife wishes to be king and queen, and the wish is granted.
    (6) ?
    (7) The castle is transformed into a little, old shack again.

- **A.** The wife makes the fish angry.
- **B.** The husband refuses to keep asking the fish for more wishes.
- **C.** The wife decides she was happy with her life before.
- **D.** The wife wishes for everything she deserves.

ELA/LITERACY PRACTICE TEST

21. This question has two parts. First, answer Part A. Then, answer Part B.

Part A
After each wish, what does the man's wife do?
- **A.** She immediately asks for another wish.
- **B.** She's happy for a while, but then she wants something else.
- **C.** She says that she's happy and grateful.
- **D.** She says she's angry that the wish isn't exactly how she wanted it.

Part B
Select the sentence from the passage that best supports your answer in Part A.
- **A.** "I did catch a flounder," said the man. "But he said he was really an enchanted prince, so I let him go." (paragraph 5)
- **B.** "When the man returned home, he found his wife crying. The stone castle had been transformed back into a little, old shack." (paragraph 14)
- **C.** "She was happy, but not for long. No matter what wishes the flounder granted, the wife always wanted more." (paragraph 11)
- **D.** "Next, the wife wished that she and her husband could be king and queen. The flounder obliged the wife again." (paragraph 11)

22. This question has two parts. First, answer Part A. Then, answer Part B.

Part A
What does the word obliged mean as it is used in paragraph 11 from the passage?
- **A.** Felt grateful
- **B.** Obeyed the request
- **C.** Denied the request
- **D.** Agreed with

Part B
Which detail best supports the answer in part A?
- **A.** "...the flounder said, "Go home, her wish has already been granted." (paragraph 13)
- **B.** "...the wife wished that she and her husband could be king and queen" (paragraph 11)
- **C.** "When the man returned home, he found his wife crying." (paragraph 14)
- **D.** Finally, she told her husband, "Just tell the fish to give me everything I deserve." (paragraph 12)

23. The passage tells about how a fisherman's wife had all her wishes given to her and then taken away.

    Pretend you are the fisherman's wife and write a letter to a friend. Tell your friend what happened to you, and the lessons you learned from this experience.

Directions: Read the passage "The Game of Kings" then answer Numbers 24 through 29.

Passage 7: The Game of Kings

1   Chess, also called "the game of kings," has been played for over 500 years. While the version of chess we play today comes from Europe, it was inspired by an even older game from India.

2   Chess is a two-player game in which one player uses white pieces and the other uses black pieces. Each piece has its own role and moves in its own unique way. For example, the bishop piece can only move diagonally. The queen can move either straight or diagonally, while the knight moves in an unusual L shape. The king can move just one square in any direction.

3   While the king can't move far, he's the most important piece on the chess board. The objective of chess is to capture the other player's king. If a player lands on another player's piece, they get to take it. But once a player lands on the other player's king, the game is over. The player who captures the king wins.

4   Chess involves strategizing and planning, so it exercises the mind. Good chess players must be intelligent and have the ability to think ahead, both skills that are also useful in life.

5   In one version of chess, called blitz chess, players have to think very quickly. In blitz chess, each player is only allowed ten minutes for the whole game. A timer runs while each player makes his or her move. When the player is done, he or she hits the timer. This stops the player's time and starts their opponent's time. If someone runs out of time during blitz chess, they lose the game.

6   Computers, too, can be trained to play chess. Since the 1970s, computers have been programmed to play the "game of kings." At first, they made many mistakes and couldn't play the game as well as humans. In 1997, a computer called Deep Blue became the first computer to beat the world's best chess player. By 2006, a cell phone could beat the best players in the world.

7   Although computers can play chess now, it's still a popular game for people to play face to face. Many people believe that chess is more than just a game. It can build thinking skills and help chess players develop abilities they can use to succeed not just in chess, but in life as well.

Now answer Numbers 24 through 29. Base your answers on the passage "The Game of Kings".

24. This question has two parts. First, answer Part A. Then, answer Part B.

Part A

Why do some people believe chess is "more than just a game?"
- **A.** They believe this because computers can play chess too.
- **B.** They believe this because chess players learn from their mistakes.
- **C.** They believe this because chess teaches players to make moves under time pressure.
- **D.** They believe this because chess teaches skills that players can use to succeed in life.

Part B

Which piece of evidence from the text best supports your answer in Part A?
- **A.** "A timer runs while each player makes his or her move" (paragraph 5)
- **B.** "Chess involves strategizing and planning, so it exercises the mind."(paragraph 4)
- **C.** "At first, they made many mistakes and couldn't play the game as well as humans" (paragraph 6)
- **D.** "Each piece has its own role and moves in its own unique way." (paragraph 2)

25. This question has two parts. First, answer Part A. Then, answer Part B.

Part A

Based on the information in the passage, how is blitz chess different from regular chess?
- **A.** Players must think strategically.
- **B.** Players must think faster because they are being timed.
- **C.** Each piece moves differently and has its own special role in the game.
- **D.** Blitz chess is a version of chess from India, while regular chess comes from Europe.

Part B

If the author wanted to organise the information in the passage using headings, which heading could the author use for the paragraph on Blitz Chess?
- **A.** Quick Thinking Under Time Pressure
- **B.** How to Learn Chess Quickly
- **C.** Computers: The Fastest Chess Players
- **D.** Winning Strategies

26. This question has two parts. First, answer Part A. Then, answer Part B.

Part A
With which of the following statements would the author of this passage most likely agree?
- **A.** Chess is too difficult for most people to play.
- **B.** The rules of chess are complicated and should be simplified.
- **C.** The king is the most important player on the board, so he should be allowed to move more than one space.
- **D.** More people should play chess to learn to think, plan, and strategize.

Part B
Which piece of evidence from the text best supports your answer in Part A?
- **A.** "Chess involves strategizing and planning, so it exercises the mind. Good chess players must be intelligent and have the ability to think ahead, both skills that are also useful in life." (paragraph 4)
- **B.** "Chess, also called "the game of kings," has been played for over 500 years. While the version of chess we play today comes from Europe, it was inspired by an even older game from India." (paragraph 1)
- **C.** "While the king can't move far, he's the most important piece on the chess board. The objective of chess is to capture the other player's king." (paragraph 3)
- **D.** "In blitz chess, each player is only allowed ten minutes for the whole game. A timer runs while each player makes his or her move." (paragraph 5)

27. This question has two parts. First, answer Part A. Then, answer Part B.

Part A
What does the word 'objective' mean as it is used in paragraph 3 from the passage?
- **A.** Not influenced by personal opinions or feelings
- **B.** Goal or purpose
- **C.** Game
- **D.** Best part

Part B
Which phrase or sentence from the passage helps the reader understand the meaning of the word 'objective'?
- **A.** "The king can move just one square in any direction."(paragraph 3)
- **B.** "...players have to think very quickly" (paragraph 5)
- **C.** "Chess is a two-player game in which one player uses white pieces and the other uses black pieces" (paragraph 4)
- **D.** "...once a player lands on the other player's king, the game is over." (paragraph 3)

28. Select the information that is missing from the sequence below.
    (1) Computers were programmed to play chess.
    (2) At first, computers played poorly.
    (3)
    (4) By 2006, cell phones could beat the world's best players at chess.

    A. Computers got better at playing chess, but they still weren't as good as humans.
    B. A computer beat the world's best chess player for the first time.
    C. The world's best chess player beat a computer called Deep Blue.
    D. Computers couldn't beat humans at chess because they couldn't keep up with the human mind.

29. Based on the information in the passage, which of the TWO following statements is NOT true about chess?

    It's a two-player game with black pieces and white pieces.
    It was inspired by a game from India.
    To win chess, you must capture the other player's king.
    In chess, each player has only ten minutes for the whole game.
    The best chess players always beat the computer.

PARCC

Grade 3 ELA/Literacy Answer Explanations

PARCC ELA Practice Test One
Answer Explanations

Unit 1

1. Answers may vary, but the table should contain phrases/words such as:

Good things about the city	Bad things about the city	Good things about the country	Bad things about the country
Brown sugar	People chasing the mice	Peaceful	Only barley and grain to eat
Dried prunes	Mousetraps	Comfortable	
Delicious cheeses	Dangerous	Safe	

(RL.3.1)

2. Part A- **B.** Part B- **A.** The mouse learns to be happy with what he has. His country life may not be filled with fine foods, but he's able to be safe, comfortable, and at peace. The quote near the end of the story supports this answer: the mouse has learned that brown sugar and cheese aren't worth more than peace, safety, and comfort. **(RL.3.2)**

3. Part A- **A.** Part B- **D.** Gnawed means chewed. While the other words would make sense in context, we know that a mouse is more likely to chew a hole in a bag than cut, tear, or make it. **(RL.3.4)**

4. Part A- **B.** Part B- **C.** He thinks it would be fun to trick the villagers. The story mentions several times that the boy thinks this joke would be fun or funny. Though it is mentioned that the villagers thought the boy did a "mean trick", there is not direct evidence in the passage to suggest that he is mean and trying to be unkind to the villagers. A student could infer that he is bored and looking for something to do, however the passage explicitly and clearly states that the boy is looking to have some fun and trick the villagers. Therefore, in part B, answer 'C' is the best choice. **(RL.3.3)**

5. Part A- **C.** Part B- **C.** At first, the villagers are caring. In the story, they're described as kind and willing to help the boy. **(RL.3.3)**

6. **1st, 2nd and 3rd choice.** The first passage teaches readers to be grateful for what they have, but the second focuses more on the dangers of lying. Both stories teach lessons, include animals and people, and are written in the third person point of view. **(RL.3.9, RL.3.6, RL.3.2)**

7. Essay answers can vary. Students should identify an important lesson in each story or one that connects both stories. Students should explain how the words and actions of the main characters are important to the overall teaching of the lessons in the stories.

For example, a student could focus on one lesson of the "Boy Who Cried Wolf" passage, which is to tell the truth. This is because, in the story, the boy lied to the villagers. Then, when he tried to tell the truth, they didn't believe him and the wolf ate all of his sheep.

Another topic a student could focus on is that both stories show it is okay to make mistakes if we learn from them. Both stories feature characters who make mistakes, but it's implied that the characters will learn from them. Additionally, these stories are retold specifically to help other people learn to avoid similar mistakes.

8.. Part A- **A.** Part B- **D** This poem is written in first person. We know this based on the speaker's use of words such as "I" and "my." **(RL.3.6)**

9. **C.** After readers are introduced to the child and the beautiful doll, the child loses the doll. When the doll is eventually found, she has changed physically: Her hair doesn't curl anymore, she's missing an arm, etc. However, the child still loves her and finds her to be the most beautiful doll in the world. **(RL.3.2)**

10. Answers may vary slightly. For the doll's appearance at the beginning of the poem, students may include that she was a "little doll," she was "the prettiest doll in the world," and/or "her cheeks were so red and white." For the doll's appearance at the end of the poem, students may mention that her hair is no longer curled, that her arm has come off, her paint is all washed away, and/or that the narrator still views her as the prettiest doll in the world. **(RL.3.1)**

11. Part A- **B.** The best answer is, "Appearance doesn't matter." The poem teaches this lesson as the child continues to love her doll and view her as "the prettiest doll in the world" despite the fact that she is now missing paint, an arm, and her charming curls. Part B- **D**. This quote supports answer B because the speaker mentions that her doll is "still" the prettiest in the world. The speaker explains that this is because of "old sakes' sake," indicating that the speaker's feelings for the doll and memories with the doll matter more than the doll's appearance.

Unit 2

12. Part A- **D.** Part B- **C.** Hummingbirds need energy because they move so quickly. The passage explains that although hummingbirds are small, they must eat a lot to help them maintain the energy to beat their wings so quickly. Hummingbirds beat their

wings as many as 80 times in a single second. **(RI.3.1)**

13. **C.** Hummingbirds and flowers have a mutually helpful relationship. The flowers feed and provide energy to the hummingbirds, and the hummingbirds help pollinate the flowers. **(RI.3.3)**

14. **2nd and 5th Choices.** The passage does not mention the honey badgers having sharp spikes. Although the picture shows a honey badger with a long furry tail, the passage does not say that this helps the honey badger be tough. The passage does, however, specify that honey badgers use their strong teeth, sharp claws, and tough skin to protect themselves and fight predators. **(RI.3.1)**

15. Part A- **B.** Part B- **B.** The main idea of this passage is that honey badgers are much tougher than they look. The passage starts off by mentioning that honey badgers are relatively small, but the rest of the passage focuses on all the way honey badgers are more tough and ferocious than one would expect. Some students might incorrectly choose choice D, but this detail only hints at one example of the honey badger's toughness. In addition, the detail only mentions what the honey badger does after it has chased a lion away. The detail does not directly describe the 'toughness' of the honey badger. **(RI.3.2)**

16. Part A- **A.** Part B- **B.** The author would agree that honey badgers can fight off much bigger predators. Although they're small, their size is not a disadvantage thanks to their arsenal of weapons and their fierce personalities. The quote about the badgers defending their homes against even horses and cows, who are much bigger than the honey badger, supports this point. **(RI.3.6)**

17. **C.** While the illustrations don't provide additional information, they do help readers visualize and understand the information in the passages about hummingbirds and honey badgers. For example, readers can see the small size of both the honey badger and hummingbird. They can see the honey badger's sharp claws and the hummingbird's hovering. **(RI.3.7)**

18. Essay answers can vary. Students should identify the special features of each creature, and explain how the features help the animal in its habitat and the pros and cons (if any) of these features for the environment.

For example, a student could discuss the hummingbird's speed and how this helps it hover over flowers to get food. In addition, a student could discuss how the shape of the bird's beak/tongue helps it get pollen. Students could explain how hummingbirds and flowers have a mutually helpful relationship. The flowers feed and provide energy to the hummingbirds, and the hummingbirds help pollinate the flowers. Students can discuss the features that make a honey badger tough (skin, claws, teeth) and which help it adapt to its habitat. These features help the honey badger get food, make a home, defend itself, and scare off predators. The badger also affects its environment in ways that could negatively impact other species - including by taking honey from bees (which also affects the beekeepers) and food from lions.

The hummingbird is more helpful to its environment. It pollinates flowers and helps them grow. Nothing in the passage suggests that the honey badger does anything helpful. An example of an appropriate student response may state: The hummingbird is more helpful to its environment. I know this because hummingbirds pollinate flowers and help them grow. On the other hand, honey badgers take food from ions and steal honey from bees.

Unit 3

19. Part A- **B.** This story teaches the lesson that we should be grateful for what we have. No matter what the magic fish gave to the wife, she was never happy and always wanted more. At the end of the story, the wife asked the fish to give her everything she deserves, so he gave her the pig-sty again. Because the wife couldn't be grateful and appreciate what she had, the fish thought she deserved nothing more. Part B- **C.** This quote best supports the answer to Part A because it shows that the wife was ungrateful and couldn't be satisfied. The other answer choices do not support the lesson that we should be grateful for what we have. **(RL.3.1, RL.3.2)**

20. **D.** After the wife's wish to be king and queen is granted, she's happy for a while. But she then wishes for the fish to give her everything she deserves. After she makes the wish, the stone castle is transformed back into a little, old shack. There is no evidence in the story that the fish became angry after the wife wishes to be queen. **(RL.3.2)**

21. Part A- **B.** The wife is happy with each wish at first, but soon she thinks of a bigger or better wish that she wants instead. Part B- C. This quote indicates that the wife is only temporarily satisfied each time a wish is granted. **(RL.3.1)**

22. Part A- **B.** Part B- **A.** The fish obeyed the wife's request. The context clue in this sentence is the word "again." Based on the fact that the fish has

obeyed all the wife's requests so far (by granting each wish), students can assume that "obliged" means to obey a request. Some students could incorrectly choose D for part A, but 'obey' is a better option than 'agree' in this context. **(RL.3.4)**

23. Essay answers can vary. The essay should be formatted like a letter, and contain an opening that introduces the character and the establishes the situation. The student should use dialogue and description (including sensory details) to tell about the events that happened and the other characters in the story. The student should include the lesson the fisherman's wife learned from her experience in the body of the letter or the conclusion.

24. Part A- **D.** Part B- **B.** Some people believe chess is more than a game because it teaches people skills that they can use to succeed in life. These skills include planning, strategizing, and thinking ahead. The text says that good chess players must be intelligent, and playing chess exercises the mind. **(RI.3.1)**

25. Part A- **B.** Players are timed in blitz chess, so they must think faster. The passage mentions that players only have 10 minutes of total playing time in blitz chess, and they lose the game if they exceed their time. (RI.3.1) Part B- **A**. Option A is the best heading as it captures specifically what players need to do to play Blitz chess. Option B is about learning the game of chess quickly, which may (or may not) happen in Blitz chess, but learning chess quickly is not the subject of the paragraph. Option D is too general and this paragraph does not focus specifically on winning strategies.**(RI.3.5)**

26. Part A- **D.** Part B- **A.** The author seems to have a favorable opinion of chess and believe that it can benefit chess players by teaching helpful life skills. For this reason, it's likely that the author would encourage more people to play chess. The author probably wouldn't criticize chess by saying it's too difficult or that the rules should be changed. Answer choice A is a quote that shows the author thinks playing chess is beneficial. **(RI.3.6)**

27. Part A- **B.** Part B- **D.** Objective means goal or purpose. The overall goal of chess is to capture the opponent's king. Readers can infer this information based on the fact that the game is over once the king has been captured, and the player who captures the king wins. **(RI.3.4)**

28. **B.** A computer, which was called Deep Blue, beat the world's best chess player for the first time. **(RI.3.3)**

29. **4th & 5th Choices.** Each player has only ten minutes for the whole game only in blitz chess. Regular chess is untimed. The passage states that computers can beat the best players in the world. **(RI.3.1)**

www.ingramcontent.com/pod-product-compliance
Lightning Source LLC
Chambersburg PA
CBHW081351080526
44588CB00016B/2455